CONTENTS

THE WORLD OF KAMEDA BŌSAI

THE WORLD OF KAMEDA BŌSAI

The Calligraphy, Poetry,
Painting and Artistic Circle
of a Japanese Literatus

Stephen Addiss

NEW ORLEANS MUSEUM OF ART
UNIVERSITY PRESS OF KANSAS
1984

The exhibition and catalog were made possible by generous grants from The Fellows and the Women's Volunteer Committee of the New Orleans Museum of Art. Additional support was received from the Mary Livingston Griggs and Mary Griggs Burke Foundation.

Exhibition schedule:

New Orleans Museum of Art	February 10-March 25, 1984
Seattle Art Museum	August 2-September 23, 1984
Helen Foresman Spencer Museum of Art, University of Kansas, Lawrence	October 14-December 31- 1984
The University of Michigan Museum of Art, Ann Arbor	February 15-March 31, 1985

Softbound copies of the catalog are available from the New Orleans Museum of Art, P.O. Box 19123, New Orleans, LA 70179. Hardbound copies are available from the University Press of Kansas, 303 Carruth, Lawrence, KS 66045.

Library of Congress Cataloging publication data.

Addiss, Stephen, 1935-
   The World of Kameda Bōsai.

   Bibliography: p.
   1. Kameda, Bōsai, 1752-1826—Exhibitions. 2. Painting, Japanese—Edo period, 1600-1868—Exhibitions. I. Kameda, Bōsai, 1752-1826. II. New Orleans Museum of Art. III. Title.
ND1457.J36K282 1984   700'.92'4   84-2004
ISBN 0-7006-0251-8
ISBN 0-89494-019-8 (paper)

Designed by Jane Thomas, New Orleans
Typography by Forstall Typographers, New Orleans
Printed in the United States by E.S. Upton Printing Co., New Orleans

Preface and Acknowledgements

Although my first journey to Japan in 1961 was as a musician, I quickly became interested in Far Eastern art, particularly ink painting and calligraphy. I was especially drawn to the brushwork of monks and scholars, and it was not long before I began to admire the landscape painting and cursive script calligraphy of Kameda Bōsai, a literati artist who had been famous in his own day but was generally neglected after the Second World War. In theory, the enjoyment of literati painting and calligraphy, the arts of the scholar, is a taste acquired after studying Chinese and Japanese culture for many years. In actuality, I was but one of a number of Westerners who found that Bōsai's lively personality was clearly expressed in his brushstrokes. I became fascinated not only by his own artistry, but also by the world of Edo period Japan in which he lived and worked. I found that Bōsai had originally wished for nothing more than to teach his pupils and serve his country, but that circumstances had forced him into another world, that of the arts, in which he excelled. His lofty spirit and technical skill in brushwork were matched by personal modesty and humor that gave a sense of life and joy to his art, a sense that is still apparent today. There are now more than one hundred examples of Bōsai's paintings, calligraphy and woodblock books in the West; with judicious borrowing from Japan it became clear that a major exhibition would be possible that could not only display Bōsai's own artistry, but also the work of his teachers, friends and pupils. My goal was to communicate the world of an extraordinary literati artist; this volume is dedicated to all those whose help I have received.

I would first like to thank E. John Bullard, Director of the New Orleans Museum of Art, and the noted collector Dr. Kurt Gitter, without whose enthusiasm and support this exhibition would not have been possible. Next I wish to acknowledge the help of friends who are modern literati in the old-fashioned style. Sugimura Eiji, librarian at Tokyo University, spent years gathering material on Bōsai, utilizing his vacations to follow Bōsai's footsteps through the Niigata area, where he uncovered new information; he then wrote a splendid book stressing the life and poetry of the master. Mr. Sugimura kindly shared his sources and assisted my research in every way, as well as contributing the following Introduction. Kwan S. Wong discussed most of the entries with me, and through his extensive knowledge of Chinese literature, painting and calligraphy he was able to decipher inscriptions in cursive script, help with translations and share the appreciation of fine brushwork. Jonathan Chaves contributed his special talents in the translation of Chinese prose and poetry, tackling some of the most difficult texts with consummate skill; his translations will be noted where they occur. Pat Fister, Research Fellow at the New Orleans Museum of Art, made many helpful suggestions on the manuscript. Further, I would like to express my thanks to Joseph Tsenti Chang, Midori Deguchi, Chu-tsing Li, Joseph Seubert, Fumiko and Akira Yamamoto and the staff members of the Spencer Museum in Lawrence and the New Orleans Museum of Art. I also wish to acknowledge the generosity of the lenders to this exhibition, who are now sharing the pleasure of owning works by Bōsai and his friends with the wider public; finally, I am grateful for the assistance of the Metropolitan Center for Far Eastern Studies and the University of Kansas for research support.

STEPHEN ADDISS

Introduction:
KAMEDA BŌSAI, THE MAN AND HIS ART
Sugimura Eiji

I began my study of Bōsai about twenty years ago, first becoming aware of his existence through reading the historical novel *Hōjō Katei* by Mori Ōgai (1862-1922). Katei had originally been a student of the Kyoto literatus Minagawa Kien (1734-1807). When Katei came to Edo, he lived in Bōsai's house. The particulars are not known, but Katei may have heard about Bōsai from his teacher Kien, whose pupil Tōjō Ichidō (1778-1857) had first studied with Bōsai. In any event, Bōsai found Katei to be an exceptionally talented young scholar, and the two became friends.

One day Bōsai obtained a rare Chinese book entitled *T'ieh-han hsin-chih* (Personal Records in an Iron Box) by the early fourteenth century writer Cheng Ssu-hsiao. Extremely disturbed by the overthrow of the native Sung government by Yuan forces, Cheng expressed his feelings in a manuscript of poems and prose which he kept in an iron box for future generations. Katei wanted to publish this volume in Japan, so Bōsai generously gave him the rare book as a gift. This story about Bōsai's personality strongly appealed to me.

Later, I read in *Taigu Ryōkan* (Tokyo, 1918) by Sōma Zaifu that Bōsai had traveled three hundred kilometers from Edo to the Gogō-an hermitage on Mount Kagami in Niigata to visit the Zen monk Ryōkan (1757-1831). Planning to offer his guest a treat, Ryōkan went out to buy some *sake*. He stopped to admire the beauty of the moon, however, and completely forgot both his errand and his guest, according to a story that is still told. There is some doubt about the credibility of this legend, but there are various other stories relating the friendship of the two men. I found myself increasingly interested in the reasons why Bōsai made the long journey to Niigata, and was thus inspired to research his life. In 1978 I published the book *Kameda Bōsai*, focusing upon his biography and poetry, and at that time I first met Professor Stephen Addiss of the University of Kansas, who was also doing research on Bōsai. Three years later I served as a guide to Professor Addiss on a trip to see many remaining paintings by Bōsai in the Niigata area, and became more aware of his importance as an artist.

Professor Addiss and I also traveled to Okayama to see works of Bōsai, Uragami Gyokudō and Kushiro Unsen. Autumn had just begun, and as we traveled on mountain roads at sunset, we could hear the symphony of insect voices. For Japanese, the chirping of insects creates a poetic mood and evokes the feeling of autumn. When listening to the voice of the *ko-orogi*, a Japanese senses the approach of fall, but Westerners may have difficulty in understanding this nostalgic feeling. The following haiku poem by the early Edo period master Bashō (1644-1694) is known by everyone in Japan:

Furu ike ya　　　　　　*An old pond—*
kawazu tobikomu　　　*a frog jumps in:*
mizu no oto　　　　　　*the sound of water*

When walking along country roads near ponds and small streams, we can often hear the sounds of frogs jumping in the water. If we pause, these frogs can be seen to float on the surface of the water, and they seem to be looking back at us.

In this Okayama locale, as the final rays of the sun floated before our eyes, we were reminded of this haiku of 1686, Bashō's forty-third year. The poet had been a lay monk of the Zen sect, influenced by Chinese Taoism, who created a new style of haiku with deep inner meanings. In this exhibition, there is a portrait of Bashō (No. 46) above which Bōsai has written a *kyōka*, a parody or humorous poem in the same form as a haiku.

Furu ike ya   *An old pond—*
 sono go tobikomu *after jumping in,*
 kawazu nashi   *no frog*

Professor Addiss showed me this poem with a smile, and asked me what I thought about its ironic meaning. At the time I had an indefinable impression. Thinking over the *kyōka* later, it seemed to me that in Bōsai's day it must have carried some feeling of resistance. In order to understand this, it is necessary to know the world in which Bōsai lived.

BŌSAI'S LIFE AND SCHOLARSHIP

Bōsai was born in Edo (present-day Tokyo) in 1752. Because he showed talent from his early childhood, he was sent to a Confucian school usually reserved for the children of samurai. In addition to finding good teachers, Bōsai met many fellow students who became life-long friends.

From the rubbing that Professor Addiss made of the wooden plaque at the Kameda family's country temple Hōshōji (see No. 6), we know that by the age of twenty Bōsai was already a fine calligrapher. It is said that he began his study at the age of five or six, and his assiduous practice is suggested by anecdotes that he used up twenty-five gallons of ink each day and rubbed his inkstone until the surface was worn away. Bōsai became expert at three forms of calligraphy—regular, running and cursive (grass) scripts. He practiced an angular form of regular script learned primarily from rubbings of ancient monuments, and also wrote out scrolls in running and cursive scripts.

In 1774 at the age of twenty-two Bōsai opened his own private academy, teaching Confucian doctrines to his pupils. Sixteen years later, the Tokugawa government, under the leadership of Matsudaira Sadanobu (1758-1829), instituted a number of reforms, primarily aimed at reconstituting the bankrupt economy. Luxuries were prohibited, and only the government-sponsored Confucianism of the Sung dynasty philosopher Chu Hsi was officially recognized. Other varieties of Confucianism were considered heterodox. Bōsai believed in the tenets of the new Eclectic school of Confucianism he had learned from his teacher Inoue Kinga (1732-1784), which were incompatable with Chu Hsi's teachings. Bōsai was in fact considered one of the "Five Heterodox Teachers" by the Shogunate. This meant that his students could not hope for government positions, and they gradually left Bōsai's tutelage to study Chu Hsi Confucianism at other academies. Without pupils, Bōsai could no longer support himself; he finally closed his school and moved to a cottage outside the city. At this time he relinquished any hopes of serving his country by teaching philosophy, ethics and statesmanship.

Returning to the *kyōka* written by Bōsai, "An old pond—after jumping in, no frog," Bōsai himself was the 'heterodox' frog. Since he did not teach Chu Hsi philosophy, he could not swim in the pond. Despite this setback, Bōsai did not find himself unpopular. On the contrary, because he was not considered to be a narrow-minded scholar, he received many requests to write book prefaces and calligraphy. He became good friends with a number of painters such as Saki Hōitsu (1761-1828), and lived the multi-faceted life of a literatus.

COMMENTARIES ON BŌSAI

Over the years, there have been a number of interesting commentaries on Bōsai as a scholar and artist, and I would like to quote a few here. The first is from the *Zokushoka jimbusshi* (Edo, 1829) by Aoyagi Tōri (1761-1839), who had also been a pupil of Kinga.

From his youth, Bōsai loved reading. His father therefore sent him to study with the famous scholar Inoue Kinga. From his youth Bōsai showed great wisdom and consideration for the common people. With his friend Yamamoto Hokuzan he insisted upon fluent and easy-to-read compositions; they took the lead in scholarship opposing the school of Ogyū Sorai. Because of this, it was said that the academic traditions of the school of Edo were complete. Bōsai became so famous there was no one who did not know of his success, but for some reason he despaired of service for the government and decided to avoid the confusion and contention of the world. He drank wine, composed poetry and followed a free-spirited literati life. In his later years he took a liking to calligraphy, and he especially excelled in cursive and regular scripts.

The next commentary is from Suzuki Tōya (1800-1852), as quoted in *Sho-en* Vol. 11 (1912).

Bōsai's calligraphy was based upon unusual and wonderful examples from old books. His cursive script is particularly modeled after the <u>One Thousand Character Essay</u> *as written by the monk Huai-su.*

It is not clear what other "unusual and wonderful" examples Bōsai might have seen, but the calligraphy of Huai-su was highly admired in Bōsai's time.

The scholar Nakane Kōtei (1839-1913) discussed the background of Bōsai's calligraphy more thoroughly in his *Kōtei gadan* (Tokyo, 1886), and also added an anecdote.

Bōsai's regular script was based upon that of Ou-yang Hsun (557-645) and Liu Kung-chuan (778-865), with angular brushwork. Bōsai's running and cursive scripts, however, are circular and fluent, quite the opposite in tone. Furthermore, his painting is pure, simple, subdued and remote, and differs from his calligraphy in flavor. Thus there are various characteristics in his art. He was such a master that ordinary literati could not compare with him.

One time Bōsai was troubled by the sickness of his wife. He received some ginseng, a very expensive medicine. After taking about half the ginseng, his wife was cured. At the end of the year, Bōsai was without funds as usual, and he wanted to buy wine. He therefore sent off the remaining ginseng to a pawnbroker with a letter asking for a loan in order to buy New Year's <u>sake</u>. *His usual letters were written so cursively that they were difficult to read, but this letter was very clearly brushed—or so said some of the malicious wits of Edo. A* <u>kyōka</u> *was circulated, teasing Bōsai:*

Bōsai no	*Bōsai's*
mushin no tegami	*begging letter*
yomeru nari	*is easy to read!*

In the *Bokudō kanbokudan* (Tokyo, 1916), the statesman and calligrapher Inugai Tsuyoku (1855-1932) wrote that he would be proud to show any Chinese connoisseur cursive script calligraphy by Bōsai and Ryōkan. In succeeding decades, however, little attention was paid to Bōsai's life or artistic accomplishments, although there have been a number of exhibitions and publications about Ryōkan. I myself am especially fond of Bōsai's running script and Ryōkan's regular script. Viewing such works, I feel peaceful and cleansed of the world's vulgarity.

Due to the activities of Professor Addiss, the New Orleans Museum of Art is presenting an exhibition centering upon the painting and calligraphy of Bōsai. Since I have long been interested in the literati arts of the Edo period, I could not be more delighted. Furthermore, the opportunity for Americans to understand an important facet of Japanese culture doubles my happiness. I send my salutations to those who have accomplished this difficult task, and I applaud their brilliant achievement.

(translation by S. A.)

THE WORLD OF KAMEDA BŌSAI

THE EARLY YEARS 1752-1799

Kameda Bōsai[1] was born on the fifth day of the ninth month of 1752 in the city of Edo (present-day Tokyo).[2] Although his ancestors had traditionally been farmers in Kōzuke (Gumma Prefecture), just north of Edo, Bōsai's father Kameda Man'emon (1711-1787) had come to the city to manage a shop specializing in products made from tortoise-shell, such as combs and hair ornaments. Since Man'emon had married at the late age of forty-two, the birth of a son was an especially happy event; Bōsai's mother Hide never fully recovered from a difficult childbirth, however, and died the following year. Bōsai's youthful name was Yakichi, and he was popularly called Bunzaemon.

When Bōsai was five or six years old, his father became owner of the tortoise-shell comb and ornament shop, which was located on Yokoyama Street in Edo's Nihonbashi section. It was at Nihonbashi that the great Tōkaidō road began, leading to the old capital of Kyoto and the merchant city of Osaka (then called Heian and Naniwa, respectively). As well as merchants plying their wares and pilgrims beginning their journeys, great processions of *daimyō* (feudal lords) with their huge retinues could be seen starting from Nihonbashi at dawn for the three-hundred-mile trek, usually on foot, over mountains and rivers, which became celebrated in the woodblock prints of Hiroshige.[3] The tortoise shells in Man'emon's shop, originally gathered from the southern island of Kyūshū, were transported up the Tōkaidō, and we can imagine the youthful Bōsai visiting the bridge at Nihonbashi to see the diversity of goods and people, including the rare visits of Europeans, coming to Edo.

Bōsai received a Confucian education, which had become standard at the time for higher-class families but was not yet as common for merchant's sons.[4] Reports of the child's exceptional intelligence and abilities at a young age still remain, and his father was prompted by praise of his son's precocious talents to ensure his serious education. The young Bōsai began, as did his peers, by reciting the Chinese classics from rote memory, a method of teaching which assumed that at some later date the child would understand the meanings of what he had learned.

Since the Tokugawa government encouraged Confucian values, Chinese literati art-forms also became widespread in the Edo period. Calligraphy in Chinese characters flourished, serving as one of the most important forms of personal expression during the eighteenth and nineteenth centuries. According to early accounts,[5] Bōsai began his study of calligraphy at the age of five or six with Mitsui Shinna (1700-1782), the leader in Edo of a Chinese style of writing that had been popularized by his teacher Hosoi Kōtaku (1658-1735). This style, based upon sixteenth and seventeenth century prototypes, had been introduced to Japan by Chinese immigrant monks of the Ōbaku sect who had left their homeland in the middle of the seventeenth century at the fall of the native Ming dynasty.[6]

Shinna's calligraphy was so popular in Edo that his seal script characters became utilized in the dyeing of fabrics, purely as formal elements of design. On a more sophisticated level, his writing of well-known Chinese texts was also highly regarded by scholars and collectors, since he combined a strong sense of structure with vigorous brushwork. His handscroll *Eight Immortals of the Wine-cup* (1770, Catalog No. 1) is an excellent example of his style. The title is composed of five large characters in seal script, testifying to Shinna's expertise in the formal elements of calligraphy. Although the characters are attenuated in a manner derived from Chinese followers of the T'ang dynasty master Li Yang-ping, Shinna allowed the rough edges of his brushwork to be seen at the beginnings and ends of certain strokes, adding vigor to his style. His seals, particularly those which follow the title, are also large and forcefully carved in the Chinese literati manner.

The main body of the text is written in a bold and dynamic running script, usually with four characters per column (for a translation of the poem, see Appendix A). In general, Shinna's format, seal script title and calligraphic style follow Ming dynasty prototypes, including the use of a seal-script title. Shinna allowed himself variations in the size of characters, in their vertical, square or horizontal emphasis, and especially in his use of line, which modulates from thick to thin in a lively but somewhat measured pacing. He was clearly confident and comfortable in writing out this lengthy poem, and was able to express his own forceful character easily and naturally through the brush. Bōsai was later to write out the same text several times (see No. 13), and it is interesting to compare the two styles. How much did the young Bōsai learn from Shinna? This is a difficult question to answer, since no works of Bōsai's childhood remain, but he must have absorbed the basic elements of calligraphy from his first teacher. In his later years Bōsai did not utilize seal script, which was one of Shinna's specialties, but Bōsai's early practice in brushwork was surely assiduous. There remain anec-

1 Mitsui Shinna, *Eight Immortals of the Wine-cup*, 1770

dotes that in his early years Bōsai would use gallons of ink each day, and that he rubbed his inkstone until it was worn out.

In 1765 the doctor and scholar Taki Morotaka (?-1766) opened a private academy, the Seijūkan, on Tenmondai street in Sakuma-chō, not far from Yokoyama street where Bōsai lived. The Seijūkan had two sections, one specializing in medical education for government and local doctors, the other focusing upon the Confucian classics, including philosophy, history and ethics. For the latter section, the outstanding scholar Inoue Kinga (1732-1784) was appointed as Chief Lecturer; he became the principal teacher of the young Bōsai, who entered the school at the age of thirteen and studied there for about ten years.

Kinga was later described in a memorial inscription by Morotaka's son Taki Rankei (1742-1801) as "a man above small matters, who liked to drink wine; no matter how much he drank his character did not change. Entirely harmonious, without sharp edges in his character, he resembled the great scholars of ancient times." When Kinga arrived at the Seijūkan, his philosophical views had just been published in the *Kinga Sensei keigi setchū* (Kinga's Philosophical Eclecticism, Edo, 1764); they represented a new and progressive form of Confucian scholarship.

Although during Japan's middle ages education

15

had largely been the domain of monks, at the beginning of the Edo period, religious leaders gradually were replaced by Confucian scholars as governmental advisors and teachers. The Tokugawa Shogunate favored their emphasis upon practical matters over the unworldly metaphysics of Buddhism. The officially approved school of Confucianism was that of Chu Hsi, the Sung dynasty philosopher who stressed the logical "examination of things" and praised loyalty to family and state. As time went by, however, this school was challenged from various sides. The Neo-Confucianism of Wang Yang-ming was adopted by some Japanese scholars; this contained elements from Taoism and Buddhism, favoring self-examination and the unity of thought and action. Other schools led by Ogyū Sorai (1666-1728) and Itō Jinsai (1627-1705) insisted upon a return to the early Confucian classics, arguing that later scholars had adulterated the original teachings. Kinga was the leader of a new trend in Confucianism, deliberately eclectic in that it borrowed certain features from all other schools. Kinga wrote:

My way of scholarship is entirely my own. Like a skilled workman attacking a tree, I take the good points [of each school] and discard the bad. The thoughts of the ancients followed their own natures, one does not need to be like others in every respect…Scholarship is based upon interpretations of earlier writings, cogitation, sincerely practicing the six arts, studying the works of Confucius, and then forming one's own understandings.

In the *Kinga Sensei keigi setchū*, Kinga compared the Chu Hsi, Wang Yang-ming and Ancient Classics schools, praising the fine points of each but writing that a blind adherence to any one of them could only hinder scholars from forming their own beliefs.

Kinga was also gifted in management, and he was soon made the administrator of the Seijūkan.[7] For the future doctors, lecturers took turns reciting from six books on medicine, including readings on medicinal herbs, causes of diseases, injuries and wounds, anatomy, clinical medicine, diagnosis, acupuncture and moxibustion. All students attended lectures on Confucianism, but Kinga allowed some to omit the medical lectures in favor of a complete Confucian education; this was the course that Bōsai followed. Kinga made his reputation as a philosopher and teacher, but he was also fond of the literary arts. Although he continued to live in the city of Edo,[8] he followed the lead of many earlier scholars in longing for a life in the countryside, in harmony with nature. Taoist-inspired ideals of tranquility and self-abnegation come forth in his poetry, exemplified in an eight-line Chinese regulated verse, *Ending Aspirations and Forgetting the Self* (No. 2).

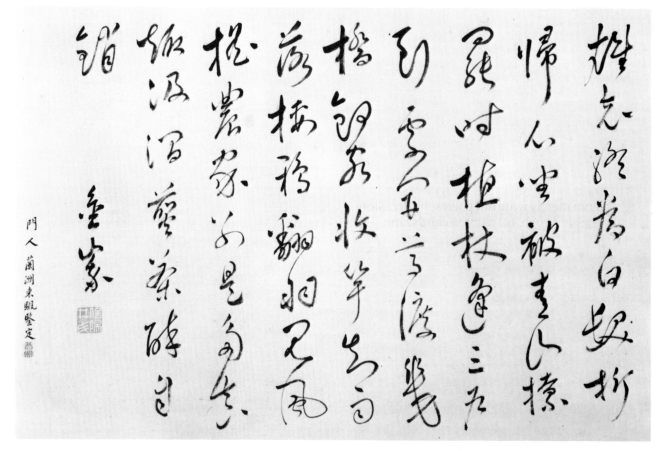

2 Inoue Kinga, *Ending Aspirations and Forgetting the Self*

Great ambition finally yields to white hair,
I long to return home to the green mountains.
Leaving, I walk with my staff to meet the three
families,[9]
Arriving, I open the wine bottle—how many
bridges have I crossed?
Out fishing, I pull in my pole as I know the
rain is coming,
I can see perching crows flutter their wings in
the vibrant wind.
Among farmers, there is true sincerity of feeling;
Ladling spring water for tea, I lose myself to
intoxication.[10]

This poem, with a closing authentication by Kinga's pupil Ranshū Tōhan (dates unknown), is written in a relaxed and informal running script. There is nothing extravagant about the calligraphy; compared to that of the professional Mitsui Shinna, it seems very modest and restrained. This is one of its literati virtues, rather than a deficiency; as one spends more time examining it, the lines and forms seem to move and dance in a non-assertive but lively rhythm. The slightly different tilts to the characters, some bending to the left, some to the right, the freedom of the brush movement and the swellings and attenuations of the lines all combine to impart to this work a fresh and almost bubbling flavor.

In literati art, there is a fine line between hiding one's skill and lacking skill, and between purposeful blandness and insipidity. As a scholar, Kinga must have had extensive training and practice in calligraphy, since writing with a poor hand would have been considered a mark of weak character. It was believed that the personality of a literatus could not help but be revealed in his writing; viewing a work by a past or present poet, artist or philosopher was tantamount to meeting him in person. The calligraphy by Kinga suggests that the outstanding scholar and famous lecturer was not stuffy or pretentious. On the contrary, his modesty and personal charm are clearly apparent in his work.

Kinga did not merely write out poems; he occasionally took up his brush to paint a landscape. His works are now very rare, suggesting that he was a true scholar-artist, painting only when he felt in the right mood to communicate his inner vision of natural harmony. His landscapes have a peaceful quality; although they lack technical finesse, they convey a spirit of relaxed ease in nature. One of Kinga's rare works to include color is *Rafting Past a Mountain Village* (No. 3). The painting is composed of the vertical thrusts of a large rock and a mountain,

3 Inoue Kinga, *Rafting Past a Mountain Village*

4 Inoue Kinga, *Drifting in a Small Boat*

against which the diagonals of the raft, path, houses and trees set the stage for the figures: a man poling a raft with a fisherman, a sage with a staff and a farmer or peddlar carrying goods on a pole balanced on his shoulders. Light washes of color and wet merging ink-tones suggest a moist and fresh atmosphere. Clusters of dots and a few interior strokes add a slight sense of bulk to the rock and mountain forms, but the effective use of blank paper gives this modest painting a feeling of spaciousness, in which mist, water and sky are as important as the forms of nature and of man.

Kinga combined his talents in poetry, calligraphy and painting in the ink landscape *Drifting in a Small Boat* (No. 4). The calligraphy, here perhaps a trifle more forceful than before, is given equal weight with the landscape, a true scholar's painting. Again diagonals are strongly emphasized: the lower rocks on the right lean up towards the plateaus atop a strangely flat mountain. Two trees seem to connect the land areas, while smaller trees and fishing nets hung up to dry in the distance add interest to the design. A sage in a fishing boat is sheltered by the lower rocks; the poem suggests he may be thinking of an absent friend:

4

> *Drifting in a little boat with someone intimate,*
> *The waters of the lake have rippled for twenty*
> *   years—*
> *I also enjoy the smoky haze from a rocky*
> *   waterfall;*
> *Sand bars to the north and south form a road*
> *   to meet my friend.*

—Painted and inscribed by Kinga for Sanshi's correction.

Unfortunately we do not know who Sanshi was, but this landscape, brushed for a friend's enjoyment, is the kind of painting that Bōsai was later to emulate. Although he went beyond his teacher in artistry, Bōsai was clearly influenced by the informal works of Kinga. In particular, Bōsai learned that restraint, modesty and a personal response to nature are more important than a concentration upon technical skill which often leads to a loss of the true literati spirit.

His years in the Seijūkan were important to Bōsai in many ways. At the school he met fellow students who were to become life-long friends, such as Katakura Kakuryō (1751-1822), whose father brought him to Edo at age eleven and entrusted him to the Taki family. When his father left to return to his home in Sagami (Kanagawa Prefecture), the young Kakuryō burst into tears. He entered the Taki household as a student assistant, and was teased by the other students as his clothes were shabby and he did not know the local customs. Since he had no money to buy books, he made copies by hand in the school library. He vowed to succeed, and in later years became famous not only for his knowledge of medicine but also for

his literary works, several of which were published during his lifetime.

Another of Bōsai's most important friends was Yamamoto Hokuzan (1752-1812), a scholar and poet who was very influential in later Edo period philosophy. Bōsai and Hokuzan became colleagues, supporting each other's scholarly as well as artistic efforts.[11] In 1773, Hokuzan wrote the *Kōkyō shūran* (Elements of Filial Piety), which was published two years later. Although not a direct pupil of Kinga, Hokuzan endorsed his teachings; in this volume he compared the views of Han, T'ang and Sung period Confucians, harmonizing their views with his own eclectic approach. Hokuzan and Bōsai became widely known as youthful exponents of this progressive trend in philosophy. They also became leaders of a new style of Chinese-style poetry in Japan, moving away from the more grandiose verse of their predecessors who had followed T'ang styles with elaborate allusions and lofty rhetoric. Instead, the young Japanese literati adopted the more personal approach of Sung and Ming dynasty masters, while accepting the best influences from many periods.

One of Hokuzan's quatrains, extolling the quiet life of a recluse, demonstrates his Taoist inclinations (No. 5).

5

> *Due to my lazy disposition,*
> *   I cannot endure the worldliness of officialdom;*
> *In order to have a peaceful life,*
> *   I plead sickness and retire to rest in my study.*
> *In my leisure,*
> *   I try to judge what's important in our lives—*
> *Only reading books*
> *   has a truly long-lasting flavor.*

The calligraphy, less developed than that of Shinna, Kinga or Bōsai, nevertheless conveys the spirit of the writer. There is a blunt forcefulness in many characters, balanced by a lighter and drier touch which saves the work from heaviness. The horizontals tend to tilt upwards to the right at a greater angle than usual, and each word is given its own clearly defined space, even when the brush does not stop between characters such as at the bottom right. One can sense that Hokuzan has no interest in elegant swirls of the brush and is not overly concerned with aesthetic effect. Although his message is one of retiring from the vexations of the world, he communicates the inner strength of his personality with a clear concentration of spirit. One senses that in an argument he would never rant or bully, but would pursue his course with a stubborn intensity of conviction which could not be dislodged. A friend like Hokuzan must have given the young Bōsai a great deal of intellectual and emotional support.

Bōsai, less affluent than most of his fellow students, brought his own lunch to school; he was considered

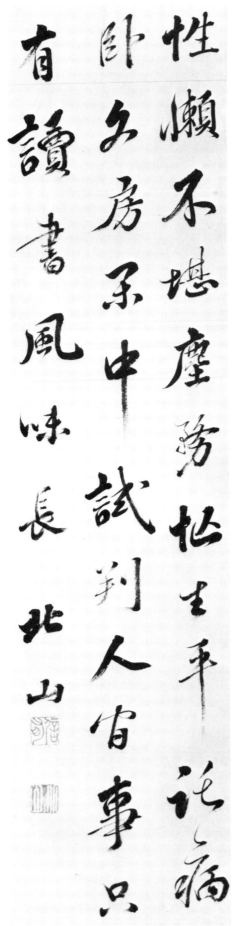

性懶不堪塵務煩
卧久房栊不中試
判人省事只
有讀書風味長　北山

odd because he disliked many forms of pickled foods, a staple of the Japanese diet. This may have prompted his studies of foods past and present, which led to several later publications. Bōsai seems to have been an exceptional student of Confucianism, mastering the difficult readings in Chinese and adding the kind of comparative evaluations that Kinga encouraged.

In the summer of 1772, the twenty-seventh anniversary of Bōsai's grandfather's death was memorialized in a Buddhist service at the family temple Hōshō-ji in Kōzuke. At this time, the twenty-year-old Bōsai wrote out the three character place-name *Tanrakuzan.*[12] The calligraphy was carved into a signboard and hung on the temple's gate (figure 1). This is the earliest extant work by Bōsai, and shows his abilities with the brush while he was still a student at the Seijūkan. The writing is more overtly decorative than his later work, which is understandable given the purpose of the calligraphy and the youth of the artist. The characters are formally arranged with an emphasis upon symmetry, especially visible in the final (left) character "mountain" but also noticeable in the placement of the three dots in the central character and the general composition of the forms throughout the signboard. There is no doubt that Bōsai was already a master of the brush; later he would hide his skill in more relaxed works which allowed his personality to come forth freely and easily. A rubbing of the calligraphy brings forth the beauty of the woodgrain as well as the high quality of the brushwork (No. 6). 6

After ten years of study at the Seijūkan, Bōsai was prepared to open his own school. In or around the year 1774, at the age of twenty-two, he established a Confucian academy in the Akasaka district of Edo. At first it was difficult for the young scholar to find students, but within a short time Bōsai became famous for his clear and brilliant lectures; during the next two decades he is said to have attracted more than one thousand followers.[13] His teachings followed Kinga's Eclectic school methodology, but incorporated Bōsai's own interpretations of the classics.

The date of Bōsai's marriage to a woman named Sae is unknown, but it probably occurred around the year 1776. Two years later their first child was born, a son named Nobu who later became known under the art name of Ryōrai.[14] Making a pun upon the family name of Kameda ("tortoise field"), his grandfather Man'emon used to tell the child that a tortoise (*kame*) has a head, a tail and four legs. If he hides all six under his shell, he will never accomplish anything, but if he exposes them all, he will find too much danger in the world. Hiding three and presenting three would be best, he advised. Ryōrai, recalling this advice later, laughed and said "that is why I

5 Yamamoto Hokuzan, *My Lazy Disposition*

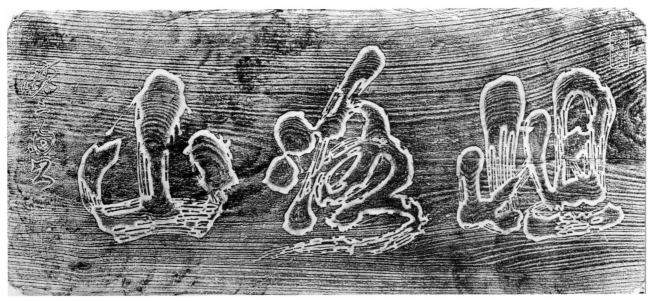

6 Kameda Bōsai, *Tanrakuzan*

always stick out my tail."[15]

As a young teacher, Bōsai devoted himself to scholarship. In 1779 at the age of twenty-seven, he wrote the *Rongo sakkai* (Explanations of the Analects), in which he annotated fifteen chapters of the Confucian *Analects.* This work, which was not published until many years later,[16] consists of a rational summary of the young scholar's views. In concert with Hokuzan's writings of the same period, Bōsai severely criticized the Ancient Classic school for its narrow interpretation of Confucianism. Ogyū Sorai, the leader of the philologist-scholars, felt that proper rites and ceremonies had been lost after ancient times. Bōsai's quick and intelligent mind could not accept the premise that two millenia of learning and scholarship should be abandoned in complete submission to early Confucian writings. Despite his personal admiration for Sorai's deep understanding of the classics, he criticized his school.

Furthermore, the young Bōsai fervently believed in his Confucian responsibility to serve his country. When it became clear in 1781 that the Shogunate was not meeting the needs of the population, Bōsai submitted a proposal towards the reorganization of the government entitled the *Fukoku zatsugi* (Miscellaneous Rules on Natural Resources).[17] In his preamble Bōsai stated that by relying upon the writings of sages from the past as well as scholars of the present day, good government could be achieved through the cooperation of the great families and the people of lesser ranks around the country.

In the twelve sections of the proposal, Bōsai mainly addressed economic questions, which were then extremely important because the government had been drifting into bankruptcy. He criticized exhorbitant taxation and the impounding of entire estates of politically questionable lords. He also pleaded for less extravagance from government, stressing the need for frugality in order to rebuild the nation's economy. He suggested new methods of accounting, and stated that abuses would continue to occur unless dishonest administrators were dismissed. He favored more careful planning of expenditures in order to eliminate waste. Bōsai also discussed the rules governing the four classes into which the population was divided: samurai-officials, farmers, artisans and merchants. He promoted agricultural reform, including suggestions for farm administrators. He wrote about the management of servants and children, and the divisions of labor in each feudal domain. He concluded with the statement that "What I have written comes from the sages of old; the contents are not new, but have been chosen from the wisdom of the past."

Bōsai's advice to the government, taking the form of "new wine in old bottles," was sincere and might have been effective if it had been put into practice;

Figure 1 Kameda Bōsai, *Tanrakuzan Signboard*, 1772, Hōshō-ji, Kōzuke

how well he understood the political realities of the day is open to question. Advice from a young scholar from a merchant family, who espoused a philosophy that differed from the approved Chu Hsi school, was not likely to be favored by the Shogunate. Bōsai's draft was completely ignored, which must have disillusioned the twenty-nine-year-old scholar.

Bōsai also suffered other disappointments at this time. His daughter Haru was born in the year 1781, but lived only three months. Two years later another daughter named Kuwa was born; she lived for three years. In 1783, a volcanic eruption caused a great fire in Edo; more than thirty-five nearby villages were buried in ash, and it is said that 40,000 people perished at this time; over a thousand homes in Edo were entombed. The stench of sulfur was everywhere, and the poor and homeless had to beg for enough food to survive. Bōsai sold his personal library to help those in need.[18]

This disaster contributed, along with bad weather and poor harvests, to the Temmei famines of 1782, 1783, 1784 and 1786. At this time, Matsudaira Sadanobu (1758-1829) wrote a draft entitled the *Kokuhonron* (Discourses on the Foundation of the Nation), criticizing the needless suffering of farmers under forced labor and suggesting administrative reforms not unlike those previously put forth by Bōsai. Sadanobu, from a family of feudal lords, had already been successful in restoring the finances of his native Shirokawa fief, and his proposals were thus taken seriously by the government which had ignored Bōsai. The recent disasters were also influential in making clear the need for reform.

In 1786, due in large part to the series of famines and economic problems, the chief advisor to the Shogun was dismissed and Sadanobu was asked to take his place.[19] At first, intellectuals of many schools welcomed the change, and offered to cooperate with the new administration. That same year, Hokuzan submitted a petition suggesting ten steps for improving the government.[20] Following the ideas of Wang An-shih of the Sung dynasty, Hokuzan believed that a scholar should understand economics and influence governmental policy, but his suggestions, like those of Bōsai before him, were ignored.

Sadanobu's primary task was the regulation of the economy, and he initiated the "Kansei Reforms" to restore the bankrupt treasury of the Shogunate. He demanded, for example, loans without interest from merchants dealing with the government. More crucial to Bōsai's future, however, were the educational reforms that Sadanobu instigated. He invited the Kyoto scholar Shibano Ritsuzan (1734-1807) to serve the Shogunate as Confucian teacher in 1788, and the following year invited Okada Kansen (1740-1816) to preside as chief scholar at the Confucian temple of the Shogunate. Both of these men strictly adhered to the official Chu Hsi school of Confucianism. In 1790, through the efforts of Sadanobu and Ritsuzan, the famous "Prohibition of Alien Teachings" was promulgated, banning other forms of Confucianism from schools maintained by the government and declaring that correct learning stemmed only from the philosophy of Chu Hsi.[21] Newer teachings which tried to "fascinate with their novelty" were "dangerous to public morality." The Wang Yang-ming school's emphasis on inner truth and the Eclectic school's stress on choosing one's own path clearly worried the Shogunate; individual morality and ethics were regarded as dangerous.

The Prohibition was by no means accepted by all scholars. Protests were sent to Sadanobu, and philosophers and literati of other beliefs continued to write and teach their own beliefs. Bōsai's friend Ōta Kinjō (1765-1825) had responded to the appointment of Ritsuzan with an ironic poem containing the lines:

Three flowers [Ritsuzan] are mistakenly promoted
*   in the jeweled garden [Shogunate]*
How can a lame horse
*   have the speed of a thousand hoofbeats?*

This inspired Bōsai to write a poem of his own, dated the first month of 1788:

Following Ōta and Expressing My Feelings

Without understanding the Way,
*   the world is empty and the Way is empty;*
Men arbitrarily pursue the Li school [Sung
*   Confucianism].*
The teacher's seat at the false gate
*   does not follow the Way of ancient Emperors,*
The true official must weep over the five suf-
*   ferings....*
At the banks of the pond,
*   ancient grasses do not find the springtime,*
Again lifting our heads,
*   we ask the heavens—why?*[22]

By this time Bōsai was an extremely successful teacher in Edo. He had attracted many intelligent students; among them was Takizawa Bakin (1767-1848), who became one of the most important writers of historical fiction of the nineteenth century. Bōsai even gave guest lectures at his old school, the Seijūkan, which was designated the official medical school for the Shogunate in 1791. Bōsai had not yet given up hope that he might directly serve the government; an anecdote relates that he was invited for an interview by Sadanobu. Bōsai usually bought his clothes in second-hand stores, and Sadanobu was extremely distressed to see that the crest on Bōsai's inner kimono did not match that on his outer robe.[23] Whether this breach of propriety was responsible for the decision not to hire Bōsai is open to doubt, because he was a leader in the Eclectic school of Confucianism which Sadanobu distrusted. Bōsai was, in fact, called one of the "Five Devils of the Kansei Period" for his "heretical" teachings.

Although Bōsai and other Eclectic school scholars continued to promote their views, it was inevitable that they would gradually lose both their influence and their pupils. It soon became apparent to students that if they wished for a career in government service, they must study with a teacher of the Chu Hsi school. In 1792, for example, the Shogunate administered an examination for potential appointees, based upon a Chinese civil service model but stressing Chu Hsi philosophy. The testing period lasted for five days.[24] The final day's examination was administered by Bitō Jishū (1745-1813), another Chu Hsi school follower recently appointed by the Shogunate. He posed the following discussion topic:

The moral duty of scholarship is very important. In the past, true learning was ignored, but in recent ages it has been studied; why did this change take place? The true learning that we follow [Chu Hsi scholarship] has been promoted by our government's educational system. In this way, samurai discipline is promoted, customs are corrected and a scholar can express his meaning without restraint.

It is clear that Chu Hsi scholarship had thoroughly penetrated the examination, and that answers from other points of view would not be tolerated.

Bōsai suffered from personal problems in these years as well as professional disappointments. His father Man'emon had died in 1787, and although Bōsai's school was still full of students that year, his family was very poor. On the night before the (lunar) New Year's day of 1788, he wrote the following poem looking forward to a brighter future.

This worthless pedant seeks any appointment,
In debt for wine, I can get no credit.
One husk of the five poverties,
A thousand worries fill my small heart.
In our poor house, my wife has become ac-
*   customed to suffering;*
I resolve to become prosperous, so our children
*   can be proud.*
*   What will the New Year bring?*
In the depths of the night, I smile in the lamp-
*   light.*

Although 1788 was not difficult for Bōsai, the following year his third daughter died and his wife became very sick. His friend Katakura Kakuryō, now a successful physician, treated Sae's illness, but she never completely recovered her health.

After the "Prohibition of Alien Teachings" in 1790, Bōsai's school gradually lost its students. At first this was not entirely unfortunate, since it left him more time for his own scholarship, poetry, calligraphy and leisurely pursuits. There is little documentation regarding Bōsai's life-style at this time, but Kakuryō wrote about a summer excursion in 1792 along the Sumida River in Edo.

In this world it is difficult to find time for an excursion, and when one has the time it is difficult to find friends, but on this day, the twenty-eighth of the sixth month, I had time and also friends, and enjoyed myself due to the kindness of Kameda Bōsai and Yoshida Kōton.

Kōton (1735-1798) had been a fellow pupil at the Seijūkan with Bōsai and Kakuryō. The Yoshida family had traditionally served in the Mito fief as doctors. Kōton's father died when he was thirteen, and he was trained to follow the profession of his ancestors. Kōton was also a scholar, writing on a number of subjects during his lifetime; he was particularly interested in later annotations of Confucian writings, and was one of the first Japanese to appreciate Yuan and Ming dynasty interpretations of the classics.[25]

In 1794, Bōsai wrote a handscroll celebrating the sixtieth birthday of Yoshida Munetsugu, also known as Joshū (1735-1797), a distinguished doctor to the Shogunate. This scroll is not only the earliest extant example of Bōsai's actual calligraphy, but also an important document relating to medical history in Japan. Furthermore, it exemplifies the literati culture of the day, in which scholarly and artistic congratulations would be bestowed upon a man reaching his "second cycle" of life.[26] The medical exploits of his ancestors and Yoshida's own attainments are extolled by Bōsai in elegant language, including sagacious comments about wordly success and inner values (No. 7); see Appendix A for the complete text.

Although Bōsai may not have been paid directly for writing this kind of congratulatory handscroll, he probably received some goods or favors in return. As a birthday greeting, it is effusive in a scholarly manner, and must have greatly pleased its recipient. As a work of calligraphy, it is important in establishing the chronology of Bōsai's stylistic development. There are many similarities to the writing of Bōsai's teacher Kinga; the characters are rendered modestly, but with a good deal of inner life, bending to the left and right with a playful, almost dancing motion. Both artists varied the sizes of their characters in running script, balancing some that are vertical with some more horizontal in attenuation. The major difference is that Bōsai's writing seems a little more fanciful and imaginative, even in this small and semi-

7

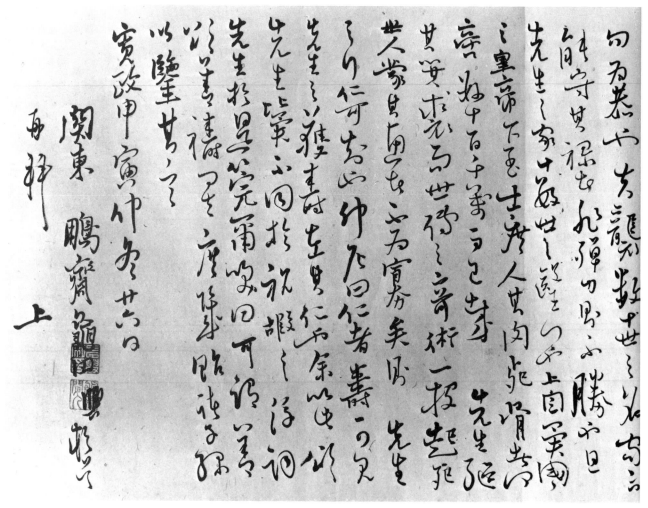

7 Kameda Bōsai, *Handscroll for Yoshida Joshū's Sixtieth Birthday*, 1794

formal work. The total rhythm of the handscroll, quite unlike that of Bōsai's first teacher Shinna, has a restrained exuberance that expresses a great deal of inner freedom and vitality. Instead of Shinna's overt dynamism, Bōsai follows Kinga's more refined style, and adds a rhythmic play of line and form that demonstrates his great talent as a calligrapher, already apparent at the age of forty-two.

During this period of his life, Bōsai's personal finances continued to worsen, due to a decline in the number of students in his school.[27] He supplemented his income by writing prefaces to books; in 1794 he wrote an introduction to a volume by his friend Kakuryō, discussing the new methods of scholarship and again stressing a wide rather than narrow approach. In the following year, Bōsai further clarified his views towards current teachings in an essay presented to Ōta Kinjō. Bōsai deplored the twisting of the truth to cater to the public, and criticized Shibano Ritsuzan for his influence in shutting out all views except those of the Chu Hsi school. Bōsai encouraged Kinjō to continue his scholarship, although it was not in fashion at the time, writing that the upright sage does not need to ingratiate himself by following the current trends. Suffering for one's beliefs and avoiding popularity is the usual course for true patriots, Bōsai concluded.

In that year of 1794 Bōsai accepted a new student who was to become one of the outstanding calligraphers of the nineteenth century, Maki Ryōkō (1777-1843, see No. 62 and No. 63). Nevertheless, the total number of pupils in the school continued to decline. In 1796 the Shogunate chose another Chu Hsi scholar, Koga Seiri (1750-1817) as a teacher; Ritsuzan, Jishū and Seiri became known as the "Three Scholars of Kansei." Bōsai's eclectic philosophy was clearly out of favor, and in 1797 he closed his school. This was a decisive moment in his life; from now on he had much more personal freedom, but he would have to earn a meagre living as best he could. He became less devoted to lecturing and more to his own research, calligraphy, poetry and eventually painting. Furthermore, his Confucian idealism towards serving the government was lost, and Bōsai turned gradually towards the Taoist ideal of living close to nature, enjoying leisure and self-cultivation.

After closing his school, Bōsai moved to Honjo Yokogawa, near the temple of Hō-onji, where he lived in a modest hut surrounded by a bamboo hedge. Although he was still within the city of Edo, it seemed like a country life. Bōsai could tell when it was time to eat lunch by the sound of the wooden fish-drum being struck at the nearby temple. In this rustic setting, he continued to write book prefaces and epilogues as well as poems, gravestone inscriptions and memorial texts. He also continued to teach a few private students. A poem by Tachi Ryū-an (1762-1844), who studied with Bōsai from the age of twelve, gives us a picture of his life at the time in "Jōzan village," a poetic name for this area.

South of Zaigobashi, his gate reflected in the
*   waters,*
Lives the teacher of Jōzan village.
After the instruction and readings have ended,
*   the children go out*
To gather fresh-water clams and return together
*   for the evening meal.*

Bōsai's own poems of this time emphasize the solitary nature of his life in the rustic simplicity of his house.

In the spring, the new greenery by the river
*   harmonizes with my gate,*
The lively young fish leave marks upon the waves.
Amidst the spring rain, my companions are gulls
*   and herons*
As I live a teacher's life in Jōzan village.

Bōsai continued his scholarship at this time; in 1798 he completed the *Shoshoku tōryō ben* (Analysis of Grains), a study of the food production and eating habits in China during the Chou dynasty. He corrected some errors of previous scholars in distinguishing various types of millet that were cultivated in this early historical era. The next year Bōsai wrote the *Daigaku shikō*, (A Personal Interpretation of the "Great Learning"). This is a commentary on one of the most important texts in the Confucian tradition; many of the debates between scholars of different schools centered upon the interpretation of

25

certain of its key passages. In particular, the virtues of "extending knowledge" and "examining things" were interpreted by philosophers of the Chu Hsi school as referring to external principles, while followers of Wang Yang-ming regarded knowledge as an innate quality, the extension of which was an internal matter. Wang's stress was upon developing one's own intuitive nature to reach a perfected state, a viewpoint influenced by the Buddhist notion of inner enlightenment. Bōsai presents both sides of the argument in some detail, offering the reader a comprehensive analysis of the different interpretations of this important text. He particularly criticizes the Wang Yang-ming school, which he feels is too close to Buddhism, but also argues that to see principles as external does not mean that a scholar must examine each and every detail of the outer world. After proper study, a kind of inner enlightenment can be reached, in which scholarship has played an important role. Bōsai did not ultimately seek to resolve all the philosophical issues, but presented differing opinions so that the reader could make his or her own evaluation.[28]

In the following year of 1800, Bōsai completed the *Kyūchū mōkyō* (Searching Through Ancient Writings), in which he traced the everchanging stream of scholarship in China through history into the Ch'ing dynasty, and encouraged the continuous study and re-interpretation of the ancient classics. He felt that Japanese officials, by regarding new learning as heretical, were closing the door to true scholarship.

Although Bōsai continued his studies throughout his life, these three volumes mark the high point of his Confucian scholarly activities. He now began to celebrate his love of the Japanese rice wine *sake*; another poem from the set of twelve about his village house refers to the "Wine Classic of the Eastern Slope" by the famous Sung dynasty literatus Su Shih.

> *Old ways, an old robe, unglazed earthenware—*
> *Leading a teacher's life in Jōzan village.*
> *Despite the bounty of spring, I can let go of*
> *   everything;*
> *From time to time I merely leaf through the*
> *   "Wine Classic."*

In these short verses, Bōsai shows his allegiance to the new informal school of Chinese-style poetry, influenced by Sung and Ming dynasty masters. Hokuzan and Kan Chazan (1748-1827) were leaders of this school in Japan, and for Bōsai, this "fresh and new" poetry became a vital part of his life. He wrote about the need to express oneself simply, honestly and clearly.

> *Days pass by, months pace onwards, in this world*
> *nothing can stop. Hearing things which touch*
> *me, the nights turn into days again. Receiving*
> *these impressions in my heart, it is like a fresh*
> *spring bubbling forth, coming from the common*
> *people and everyday life without exhaustion.*
> *True poems are made from the environment*
> *and from individual circumstances, and do not*
> *need flowery language or ornamental styles. In*
> *the long run, copying the past is not the way*
> *to write good poetry.*

Bōsai's Chinese-style poems were becoming celebrated in Edo for their freshness, honesty and informality. Several short verses from this time show how he accepted his new life:

> *Success and failure are neighbors*
> *   and share a common border;*
> *My drunken village is the true paradise.*
> *   This leisure has no honor or shame,*
> *Why worry about serving the world*
> *   or hiding from it?*

One Smile

> *One smile—I've lived foolishly for fifty years;*
> *My literary works are not worth half a penny.*
> *I return to search for a secluded dwelling and*
> *   bolt the door—*
> *When rain beats on the hills,*
> *   I listen to the raindrops and sleep.*

Leisurely Self

> *A leisurely existence with no possessions is an*
> *   ancient life-style;*
> *Leisure means having no place to show off to*
> *   other people—*
> *I eat rice made from wheat flour and burn*
> *   incense;*
> *When tired from eating, I sleep;*
> *   when it's time to wake, I drink tea.*

There are several anecdotes remaining from this time about Bōsai's poverty and his lack of concern for worldly cares. One relates that he returned naked from a visit with a friend. His mother-in-law told him he was indecent, so he explained that on the way home he had accidently slipped and fallen into a ditch. Since his kimono had then smelled foul, he had thrown it away. He had no change of clothes, but he said that since he had been born naked there was no disgrace in being naked now.[29] Bōsai's son Ryōrai later commented that as a child he had only one *yukata* (robe), so when it was being cleaned he was always naked.

The family's small income came entirely from Bōsai's writing fees. When a visitor requested Bōsai's calligraphy or a preface to a book, he was said to turn the payment over directly to his wife or mother-in-law. They were all open-hearted, and if someone asked them for money, Bōsai's family would give what they had. Strictly speaking, a literatus was not supposed to sell his works if he wished to maintain the proper amateur spirit, but Bōsai had little choice. He felt that living among farmers, he farmed with his brush;[30] any money he earned could be given away or used to buy wine and food for his family and visitors.

Bōsai from this time onwards was especially admired by the townsfolk. While other scholars and calligraphers were favored by the samurai-officials who comprised the upper class of Edo, he was known as a "downtown" master beloved by the common people. It was said that his house was frequently crowded; Bōsai would stay up drinking with his guests until they went to bed, then he would remain awake to study until dawn. Whether these stories are strictly true or not, they give a picture of how Bōsai was seen by his contemporaries. Bōsai's view of himself emerges from his poetry.

> In my house, I have not one penny,
> But when I have wine I'm on top of the world.
> Taoist sages unify their intentions with what
>   happens naturally;
> Content with what he has, even a poor man
>   becomes an immortal.

As Bōsai neared the age of fifty, he turned not only to wine and verse, but to painting as well.[31] His next years were devoted to the arts and to travel; the new sights certainly stimulated his painting and poetry, and offered him occasions to practice his already well developed skills in calligraphy. His philosophical teachings and scholarly works had not been well accepted in late eighteenth century Japan; undaunted, he became one of the great literati artists of the early nineteenth century.

---

1 There is some question whether the name should be pronounced Bōsai or Hōsai. Family tradition and the 1821 book *Myōmyōkidan* (see No. 36) give Bōsai as the correct reading.

2 Some sources suggest that he was born in Chiyoda village in Kōzuke where his father had lived before moving to Edo. The most thorough scholarship, however, has been done by Sugimura Eiji in his book *Kameda Bōsai* (Tokyo, 1978), and for the following biographical information I have relied primarily upon Mr. Sugimura's research. Quotations not otherwise identified are from this source.

3 See Stephen Addiss, ed., *Tōkaidō: Adventures on the Road in Old Japan* (Spencer Museum, Lawrence, Kansas, 1980) for further discussion of the Tōkaidō road and its art.

4 Although merchants were officially considered the lowest class, they gradually accumulated enough wealth to partake of many perquisites of the samurai-officials. Confucian education had at first been primarily limited to the highest class; by the early nineteenth century it was becoming more available for the sons of wealthy merchants.

5 See "Kameda Bōsai," *Kensei bijutsu*, No. 134 (1919), p. 22.

6 For a further account of the monks and their calligraphy, see Stephen Addiss, *Ōbaku Zen Painting and Calligraphy* (Spencer Museum, Lawrence Kansas, 1978).

7 The school was built with a front gate for official visitors, a middle gate for students to enter, and a back gate for servants. Government officials entered by a dock on the canal that passed the school. There was a large lecture hall with a platform for the teachers, smaller classrooms, an office for meeting guests, a library and a study hall. The latter was divided into three sections, one for future doctors who would serve the central government, one for medical students who would serve feudal lords and one for those to serve the townsmen.

8 Kinga left the school in 1771 to give special lectures for the feudal lord of Ōshū, but he preferred teaching at the Seijūkan and soon returned.

9 A reference to the three families of Ch'u who eventually became important enough to overthrow the Ch'in dynasty.

10 All translations are by the author unless otherwise noted.

11 For anecdotes about Bōsai and Hokuzan, see Nishikawa Gyokko, "Kameda Bōsai Sensei den" (The Life of Kameda Bōsai), *Kōzuke oyobi Kōzukejin*, No. 79 (November, 1923), p. 34.

12 This signboard still hangs in the gateway, although the temple itself is now only opened for the occasional visits of a traveling monk.

13 See Karaki Junzō, *Myōmono no keifu* (Tokyo, 1964), p. 153.

14 Some sources list Ryōrai, probably erroneously, as Bōsai's adopted son.

15 From the *Denjitsu shiki*, quoted by Sugimura, op. cit., p. 229. Ryōrai had the nickname of "Sansō" (Three Hiding).

16 It was included in Bōsai's *Zenshindō ikkagen* (One view from the Zenshindo, Edo, 1823).

17 It was later published in the compilation *Nihon keizai sōsho* (Japanese Economic Series), Vol. 19 (1915).

18 See Saitō Shiseki, "Kameda Bōsai to Saitama bunka" (Kameda Bōsai and Saitama Culture), *Musashino shidan*, Vol. 2, Nos. 3-4 (1953), p. 48.

19 He officially received this position in the sixth month of 1787; thus, by the age of thirty he had achieved the pinnacle of governmental power.

20 These included finding the most talented men to serve, holding honest discussions, improving official ceremonies, setting up training institutes in the villages with Confucian lectures, utilizing elder scholars for teaching the young, regulating public ostentation and morality, considering the use of the "wondrous instruments" brought to Nagasaki by Dutch traders, encouraging filial piety, systematizing recommendations and examinations for those who wished to serve the government and regulating the economy to prevent famine.

21 The text of the "Prohibition" is given in Tsunoda et. al., (ed.), *Sources of Japanese Tradition* (New York, 1958), pp. 502-3.

22 More than two hundred and fifty of Bōsai's poems were published in the *Bōsai Sensei shishō* (A Selection of Bōsai's Poems, Edo, 1822). Along with his prose, they have recently been republished through the efforts of Mr. Sugimura in the *Kameda Bōsai shibun-shoga shū* (Collection of Bōsai's Prose, Poetry, Calligraphy and Painting, Tokyo, 1982).

23 This story is reported in Nakane Kōtei, *Kōtei gadan* (Elegant Discussions by Kōtei, Tokyo, 1886), p. 25.

24 The first was devoted to questions on Chu Hsi's *Lesser Learning*, the second on the *Four Books*, the third on the *Five Classics*, the fourth on history and the fifth on current problems.

25 In 1823, twenty-five years after Kōton's death, Bōsai contributed a preface to a collection of Kōton's essays, commenting on his love of art and scholarship.

26 The traditional Chinese yearly cycle lasted sixty years, and it was felt that a man began a new life at that age, since he was now presumably free from the cares of raising a family and earning a living.

27 His wife was sick in 1793 and 1794, and it was at this time that he acquired the ginseng to cure her. His letter asking for money for *sake* from a pawnbroker, using the remains of the ginseng as collateral, occasioned the humorous poem quoted in the Introduction.

28 I am indebted to Jonathan Chaves for his comments on this volume.

29 For this and the following anecdotes, see Harada Kampei, "Kameda Bōsai ryakuden" (An Abridged Life of Kameda Bōsai), *Bokubi*, Vol. 148 (1965), p. 33.

30 One of the names he used on his seals was "Ink farmer," see Appendix B.

31 Although no paintings survive from this time, Bōsai's skill only a few years later suggests that he was developing a personal style and technique during these years.

THE YEARS OF TRAVEL
1799-1812

One advantage of closing his Confucian academy was that Bōsai was free to travel. Although he probably earned very little money at this time, he had many friends and patrons who made his journeys possible. For example, in 1799 the merchant Hamaguchi Gihei, who ran a soy brewing business, invited Bōsai to visit his ancestral home in Hiromura in the Province of Kii (Wakayama Prefecture). This involved a journey down the Tōkaidō to Kyoto and Osaka, and then a boat ride from Osaka Bay. Hamaguchi no doubt bore the expenses, in return for Bōsai's company and very likely some poetry and calligraphy; eventually Bōsai also wrote a grave inscription for Hamaguchi at the request of his family.

The journey occupied the entire autumn of 1799; Bōsai left Edo in the sixth month and did not return until the ninth. In Kyoto he met with a former pupil, Tōjō Ichidō (1778-1857), who had been a close friend of Bōsai's son Ryōrai.[1] Ichidō, from a family of farmers and *sake* brewers, had come to Edo at the age of eight after his father's house had been destroyed by fire. He remained a pupil of Bōsai from 1786 until 1793, when he went to Kyoto to study with Minagawa Kien (1734-1807), perhaps because of the lack of opportunities for students of the Eclectic school in Edo.[2] Bōsai was happy to see his former pupil again, and together they spent enjoyable times with Kien, who was a scholar, poet, painter and calligrapher, and also a frequent visitor to the entertainment districts of Kyoto. Through the friendship of Kien, Bōsai undoubtedly met many of the artistic leaders of the old capital. In particular, he would have been able to meet former pupils and other painters influenced by Ike Taiga (1723-1776), whose Nanga style was very prominent in the late eighteenth century. Whether at this time or at some later date is not certain, but Bōsai wrote a poem as a colophon for one of a set of four small Taiga paintings, originally on panels, that were made into an album by their new owner in 1799.[3] *Fishing Boat at the Reed-covered Bank*, the landscape for which Bōsai wrote a colophon, is one of Taiga's deceptively simple works, depending on soft brushwork and adroit placement of elements to suggest nature's unpretentious harmony (No. 8).

8

Bōsai's poem, written in energetic regular script with occasional characters in running script, begins with the image of the solitary fisherman, but ends with a more complex allusion (No. 9).

9

In the cold river, near a lone fishing boat,
Withered reeds rustle and murmur in the wind.
The fisherman pulls in his line, but where will
he return?
He should go to the "Tide Society" meeting.[4]

Since Bōsai gives the title of the painting after his poem, it is possible to compare his calligraphy directly with that of Taiga in the same four characters. In Bōsai's case, they begin with the final word in the third column from the left, and continue with the first three words of the penultimate column. Compared with those of Taiga, Bōsai's characters tilt further upwards to the right, and were brushed with thinner and drier lines. They are more angular in structure, and seem to have been executed with greater speed and exuberance. Taiga's calligraphy adds a sense of weight to his painting, which otherwise might have become too slight. Bōsai, on the other hand, gave free reign to his vivid energy.[5]

On the journey to Kii, Bōsai wrote several poems based upon scenes and famous places that he visited. Near Lake Biwa's northern shore lies the island of Hanjūyama, which inspired the following lyric.

Full Moon at Hanjūyama

One peak seems to descend amidst the flow,
At its summit is a silver tower.
Suddenly I know this is the cave of a Taoist wizard
Upon the island of a goddess.
The autumn moon stirs the gentle waves,
Evening clouds float like curling snail shells.
Waves move as if they were coming to meet me.
The goddess prepares the boat of the immortals.

After a leisurely visit with the Hamaguchi family in Hiromura, during which time Bōsai wrote out an elegant name for his host's garden, he set out on the return voyage to Edo. Again the splendid scenery captured Bōsai's attention.

Old Fort at Hachiōji

The polished mossy cliffs seem to call for my
inscriptions,
Stubborn clouds gather together, chilly and cold.
Amidst a single grove of frosty leaves, a flag
flutters,
The autumn wind shudders like war drums in

8 Ike Taiga, *Fishing Boat at the Reed-covered Bank*

the myriad valleys.
Grass grows wild in the ruined fort, foxes have
dug burrows,
Deer tracks cover the dry canal beds.
Springs gush forth furiously again;
As rain pours down on the cold mountain,
I have lost my way home.[6]

The most imposing sight of Bōsai's entire journey
may have been that of Mount Fuji. Bōsai was able to
ascend a two-storey pavilion, built in imitation of a
Chinese tower, to view the mountain and its nearby
lakes at daybreak.

Viewing Mount Fuji at Dawn from a
Seaside Tower

Over richly flowing waters, I view the limitless
expanse,
The dawn sky makes all things brilliant.
The mountain colors rejoice at the rising of the
sun,
The wind ruffles the surface of the waters.
Nearby sails break up the unity of the arriving
clouds,
Distant birds provoke the shifting mists.
I dream of catching a sea-tortoise on a fishing
pole—

Waking, I can see ten thousand feet of snow.
No dust can stain the great ocean,
The magnificent peak can be seen in the palm
of the hand.
At daybreak I ascend a tower to admire the dawn,
And I am able to capture the freshness of the
sunrise.

On his return to Edo, Bōsai again wrote out a series
of texts and inscriptions upon request. His friend
Tanaka Gyokuhō (1759-1828) visited him on New
Year's day of 1800 to request a preface to the *Bunrin*
tekiyō, a new anthology of literature, testifying to
Bōsai's increasing fame as a prose and poetry expert.
Later that year Bōsai was shown a painting by his late
teacher Kinga, and he inscribed it with the following
quatrain, showing his continued devotion to the
philosopher and artist:

Old man Kinga, after discussing the classics,
Painted "Fishing Alone on the Autumn River."
The ink is not yet dry, but he has already passed
away:
Finishing this inscription, I return alone with a
long sigh.

29

At about this time, Bōsai moved his home in Edo to Bakurochō, but in 1801 he moved again to the Kanasugi district in northeast Edo, where he could lead a rural life within the city limits. In this year he reached the age of fifty by Japanese count. Considering himself one of the most strange and useless people in the Kantō (Tokyo area), he wrote the following self-depreciating poem.

For laziness and carelessness, no one can compare.
With the craziest man in the Kantō.
My eyes bleary, full of songs, what course can I pursue?
After half a lifetime, at age fifty everything is perfect.

Bōsai seems to have enjoyed his leisure; that year he made a journey to Kiryū (Gumma Prefecture) at the invitation of a textile merchant who admired Bōsai's poetry. Later in 1801 Bōsai wrote out a text for the epitaph of Taki Rankei, the Seijūkan doctor and seven-string *ch'in* player who had previously written the epitaph for Kinga.

Bōsai fully appreciated the peaceful nature of his Kanasugi home, as the following two poems suggest.

Autumn Day at My Rural Home

Rural huts girdle the mountain-side,
Brushwood doors open out to a meandering stream.
In the evening sunlight, among golden oranges and green bamboo,
The wild birds, with no people about, can fly freely.

Firmly shutting my door, just being lazy,
I sit by my bamboo window; enjoying old things, I forego poetry.
The fallen leaves pile up before my gate, Lying down,
I listen to the chanting of mountain monks on their travels.

Bōsai's interest in painting must have been growing at this time, since two of his closest friends from this period onwards were great masters of the brush. One was Sakai Hōitsu (1761-1828), who came from a samurai family but did not wish to follow the life of his ancestors. In 1793 he retired from his hereditary position, entering the Buddhist order as a way of escaping from burdensome official duties. As Hōitsu was also living with his courtesan lover at this time, he did not escape criticism; a poem he wrote expresses his feelings clearly:

Itō tote   *Because I dislike [ceremonies]*
hito no togame so   *people speak ill of me—*
utsusemi   *amidst the world*
yo ni itowareshi   *like a cicada leaving its body,*
konomi narisheba   *I am despised because of my tastes*

Hōitsu was skilled at poetry, calligraphy and especially painting. He studied under various masters until finding his true metier in the decorative art of the Rimpa school, which he revived brilliantly following a period of decline. Patterning his style upon that of Ōgata Kōrin (1658-1716) and producing several woodblock books of Kōrin's designs, Hōitsu established himself as the leading nineteenth century Rimpa master. In the free artistic atmosphere of Edo, the literatus Bōsai and the decorative painter Hōitsu became lifelong friends.[7]

Bōsai's other artistic friend from this time onwards was Tani Bunchō (1763-1840), considered a Nanga master but actually an expert at almost every painting subject and capable of a wide diversity of styles. Bunchō was already well on his way to becoming the most popular artist in Edo, with a large studio and several hundred students. In the summer of 1802, Hōitsu, Bunchō and Bōsai were invited to visit Wakashiba, where there was a fine collection of old paintings in the local temple. They journeyed in part by boat, eliciting a poem from Bōsai.

Down the Tonegawa

Ten thousand miles of blue river,
flowing ten thousand miles;
The water is high with sudden wind,
seagulls lamenting,
Tossed by the wind, the boat moves swiftly,
running from the billows—
Trees on shore retreat,
mountains ride the boat.

In this poem, the intensity of vision represents the actual imagery seen from a boat bouncing high upon the waves.

Reaching Wakashiba, the three friends viewed the paintings at Kinryūji, a temple founded in 1331. Although there were several early Buddhist scrolls, they were most interested in a portrait of Su Shih, painted by a little-known artist named Kōgetsu Dōbun. Bunchō made two copies of this portrait, giving one each to Hōitsu and Bōsai.

Three months later, Bōsai took a boat journey to Shimosa (Chiba Prefecture), where in 1564 a great battle had been won by an army led by the flight of a white bird. Bōsai could not help but recall the "Red Cliff" poems, written by Su Shih in 1082 while visiting an area where a Chinese battle of 208 had taken place. Noting that 1802 was the anniversary of Su Shih's poems according to the Chinese 60-year cycle, Bōsai addressed the following homage to the Chinese master:

Floating at the Base of White Bird Hill,
1802 Ninth Month,
Following the Journey by the Red Cliff

This is the anniversary of the year
When from ancient times a voice has flowed
*   with the river;*
Mountains resound, valleys answer this year's
*   ululations,*
The moon is white, the wind is pure for this
*   evening's journey.*
The remnants of a fortress loom over a thousand
*   feet of shore,*
The faint sound of a bell seems smothered in
*   the dampness.*
As we look at the frosty sky, the evening is half
*   gone—*
A solitary crane, intersecting the sky, passes
*   our small boat.*

In this poem, Bōsai shares with Su Shih the wonder over how the passage of time can diminish even the greatest of human events. He suggests that ultimately Su's poem will live on when military triumphs are forgotten. The solitary crane, which in Su's poem had been a Taoist wizard, may represent Su Shih himself; since the crane is also a symbol of longevity, Su lives on in the memory of those who are still moved by his life and art.

Bōsai did not abandon his Confucian studies, although they were no longer the major element in his life. In late 1802, he wrote a preface for Ōta Kinjō's *Kinjō hyakuritsu* (Kinjō's Hundred Laws), a further criticism of Chu Hsi philosophy. The following year Bōsai was invited to speak at a new lecture hall in Saitama along with other well-known scholars. At the same time, Bōsai was becoming more involved with the arts; his two earliest extant landscape paintings date from 1803. One of these remains in a collection on Sado Island, Japan. Another, dated to the twelfth month,[8] is a powerfully conceived work in the true scholar-painter tradition (No. 10). Bōsai's conception of landscape art has its roots in the styles of the Chinese Yuan dynasty masters as interpreted by Ming painters of the Wu school.[9] The refined calligraphic brushwork and the lofty spirit of Bōsai's landscape shows his reliance upon this literati tradition. Furthermore, both the general composition of Bōsai's painting and the diagonally leaning mountain forms are reminiscent of the ink landscape of Kinga (see No. 4). Bōsai's scroll, however, is more

10

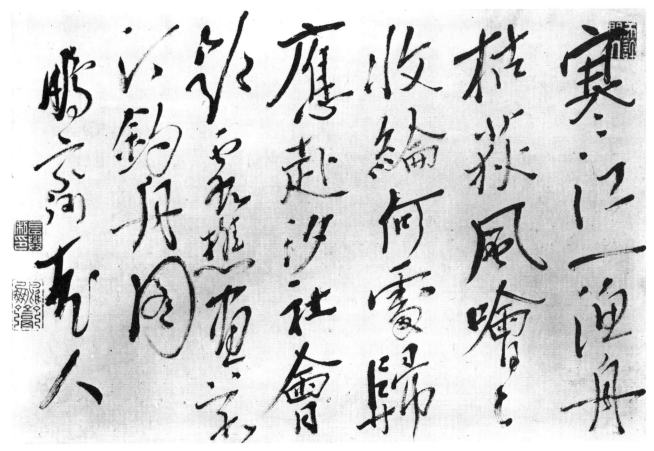

9 Kameda Bōsai, *In the Cold River*

10 Kameda Bōsai, *Truly a Dream*, 1803

imposing and includes light washes of color. The painting is also enriched by Bōsai's poem, written in fluent, almost quirky cursive script.

Fifty-three years—truly a dream!
A useless bookish old man in a rustic cottage,
Sitting alone by my secluded window with no
*   one to talk with,*
I pick up the brush to depict mountains on
*   this paper.*
*   —Painted and inscribed by Bōsai, the twelfth month of*
*   1803*

Unlike more professional artists, Bōsai did not complicate his mountain forms with inner texture strokes (*ts'un*) and the result is both majestic and fanciful. The peaks are beyond rational belief, yet their serene emptiness gives them a sense of floating weightlessly in space. The countering diagonal of a larger mountain, rendered almost invisibly in light blue wash, adds a final touch of balance to this large and impressive work. Although his later landscapes might show a slightly more disciplined use of line, this early painting demonstrates that by 1804, Bōsai's style was already well established; his later paintings exhibit similar compositions and the same basic conception of brushwork.

Although Bōsai was only beginning his activities as a painter, he was already well known as a calligrapher. One of his works from this time[10] is an impressive single line of calligraphy: *The Ultimate Principle is Beyond Words* (No. 11). This may seem an unusual message from a scholar, and suggests a mystical, perhaps Taoist, side of Bōsai's character.[11] Perhaps his unhappy experiences as an idealistic young teacher led Bōsai to distrust words, but he also knew that art could reach deeper into the human spirit, less distorted by rationalizations. The calligraphy, in a combination of regular and running scripts, is powerfully and deliberately awkward. Although the line is generally even in width, it does not curve gracefully but bends in angular thrusts to produce a sense of dynamic movement. At times the brush moved so quickly that one may see the paper through the strokes ("flying white"), although the ink is generally dark and rich in tonality.

A single line of calligraphy demands not only well-composed characters, but also a unified compositional relationship between them. Here Bōsai has given the first word a vertical emphasis. The second word is a single extended horizontal stroke meaning "one." Next comes another vertically elongated character meaning "principle," followed by the word for "not" which has been compressed horizontally. The final two characters meaning "words" or "literature" fit

11 Kameda Bōsai, *The Ultimate Principle*

into the column with varying degrees of tilting, so that the entire calligraphy has a rhythmic balance with a great deal of internal variety. Another aspect of this diversity can be seen in the horizontal strokes. For the second word ("one") the line rises slightly upwards to the right. In the fourth word ("not") the top line is strictly horizontal, while the widest line below it is at a strong diagonal, echoed by the horizontal line near the top of the next character. The tensions and the resolutions suggested by these changes give the work its individual character. The signature to the left sets off the dynamism of the larger characters by its lighter and more curvilinear brushwork.

Another single-line calligraphy, perhaps slightly later in execution, has a more Confucian tone: *The Virtuous Man Patiently Endures for Fifty Thousand Years* (No. 12). This work seems a little less energetic, due to the larger number of characters and their relatively equal size and spacing. Yet the various tilts to the different words, including the changing angles of the horizontal strokes, mark it as a work of Bōsai's early maturity. The artist has chosen an absorbent paper so the beginnings of each character show fuzzing ink, in contrast to the "flying white" at the end of each word. The penultimate character leans to the left, so Bōsai has begun the final word with a tilt to the right. This gives the calligraphy a sense of total design which is balanced by the freedom of the brushwork. The even spacing may reflect the sober sentiments expressed, in contrast to the more Taoist meaning of the previous calligraphy, but the energy of Bōsai's brushwork is still apparent in the strongly angular forms and the somewhat gnarled spontaneity of the work's total impact. To the left of the calligraphic phrase Bōsai has written that it was originally composed by the former abbot of the Kōundō, the Zen master Issan, referring to I-shan I-ning (1247-1317), who came to Japan in 1299. I-shan was a master calligrapher and scholar as well as a Buddhist monk, and he helped to spread Zen, Neo-Confucianism and literati culture in his new homeland.

There is an amusing anecdote regarding Bōsai's fame as a calligrapher in the *Ne monogatari* (Dream Story) of the haiku poet Sokei. It recounts an incident at a party where the guests included Bōsai and his friend the poet and man-about-town Ōta Nanpo, also known as Shokusanjin (1749-1823). Someone asked Nanpo for an impromptu verse about Bōsai. Taking up the brush, Nanpo immediately wrote three lines in haiku form.

12

Oto ni kiku
dai Bōsai ga
fude no ato

The brush traces
of the well-known name of
the great Bōsai—

12 Kameda Bōsai, *The Virtuous Man*

Another guest remarked that this sounded like praise; it might be more fun if the poem were an insult. Thereupon Nanpo added a couplet, changing the poem into the classical *tanka* form:

sansui tengu   *are like the writings of*
kaita yō nari   *a penniless goblin!*

This was highly appreciated by all those present, including Bōsai. At least the penniless description was no doubt close to the truth.

In 1804 Bōsai went on another journey, this time taking his wife with him, rather an uncommon courtesy in Japan at the time.[12] They first stopped at Kanazawa to view a strange rock at the Kinryū-in. The shape of this stone resembled a black kite, and it was reported to have flown to this spot at some previous time; perhaps it was a meteorite. Bōsai was inspired to compose a light-hearted poem.

Hiraiseki ["Flying-here-stone"] on the Outskirts of Kanazawa

Where did this stone come from?
Its journey has brought it to this hillside.
Whatever comes here must surely leave again,
Where will it fly to next?

Bōsai has gently personified this stone, perhaps comparing it to himself. His own fortune was better than that of the rock, for it shattered during an earthquake the following year and could never fly onwards. In 1807 Bōsai heard of this misfortune and wrote another quatrain:

The rock has lost its way home,
The stone has fallen and has no way to return.
It's a pity to know that it lies under brambles—
Remaining forever, never to fly again.

Bōsai and his wife continued on to the celebrated beauty spot of Enoshima, enjoying the beach and watching the shell-gatherers. Unfortunately, Bōsai became sick with what he called a "blood disease" (perhaps a stomach ulcer), which caused him to vomit blood. This was serious enough for him to give up *sake* for a time. Instead, he drank an extract of lotus root as medicine.[14] Bōsai was forced to postpone an invitation from his friend and former pupil Yajima Kazue (1775-1832) for a longer journey to Sado Island, and returned to Edo and wrote another poem extolling the beauties of nature; the experience of traveling must have encouraged both his poetry and his painting.

The breath of the immortals carries me over layered mountain peaks;

To the east, the blue ocean spreads out before my eyes.
Through the deep mist, sharp peaks rise up a thousand feet,
In the blue vastness, a great island appears like a cannonball.
To one side is a jeweled world of snow-colored flowers,
To the other, ocean waves dance on golden wings.
Aromatic trees which have never been felled grow in the sacred grotto;
Pines billow over the entire mountain in the cool summer breeze.

The following year, Bōsai oversaw the publication of his book on Chou dynasty foods, *Shoshoku tōryō ben,* and continued to write prefaces, epitaphs and painting inscriptions upon request.[15] In 1806, his son Ryōrai at the age of twenty-eight married the seventeen-year-old Ito, daughter of Tsugawa Hisakatsu. In the same year Bōsai wrote prefaces for two books on Chinese poetry. One was the *Bantō shishū* (Selection of Late T'ang Poems) edited by his friend Tachi Ryūan, the other a translation of a book by the important Ming dynasty poet and critic Yuan Hung-tao.[16] The latter book in particular became an important influence upon the new wave of Chinese-style poets in Japan, although T'ang verse remained very popular.

While living in Kanasugi, Bōsai wrote out the poem *Eight Immortals of the Wine-cup,* the same text chosen by his teacher Shinna in 1770 (see No. 1). Bōsai utilized the format of a pair of six-panel screens, giving his calligraphy great visual impact (No. 13); See Appendix A for a translation of the poem. He wrote both the title and the poem in cursive script, but the same features we have seen in his regular and running script calligraphy are apparent. The compositions of the characters are forceful, sacrificing grace for a powerfully unified sense of dynamic boldness. Compared with Shinna's calligraphy, the main difference is in brush movement; some critics might regard Bōsai here as undisciplined, yet the total effect is vigorous and the brushwork is always under control. Characters lean and tilt to the left and right, sometimes seeming to run together and sometimes allowed more individual space. There is a unique combination of swirling activity and occasional simplicity in this calligraphy that suggests both complexity and spontaneous joy. One unusual feature is that Bōsai, towards the end, lost track of where he was in the poem; he skipped one couplet entirely and wrote the following couplet twice. Thus the two penultimate panels contain the same two columns of seven characters each. Was Bōsai himself somewhat drunk when he brushed this paean to wine? He signed the screens "The drunken scholar of Kanasugi, old man Bōsai." In any case, viewing two panels with exactly

13

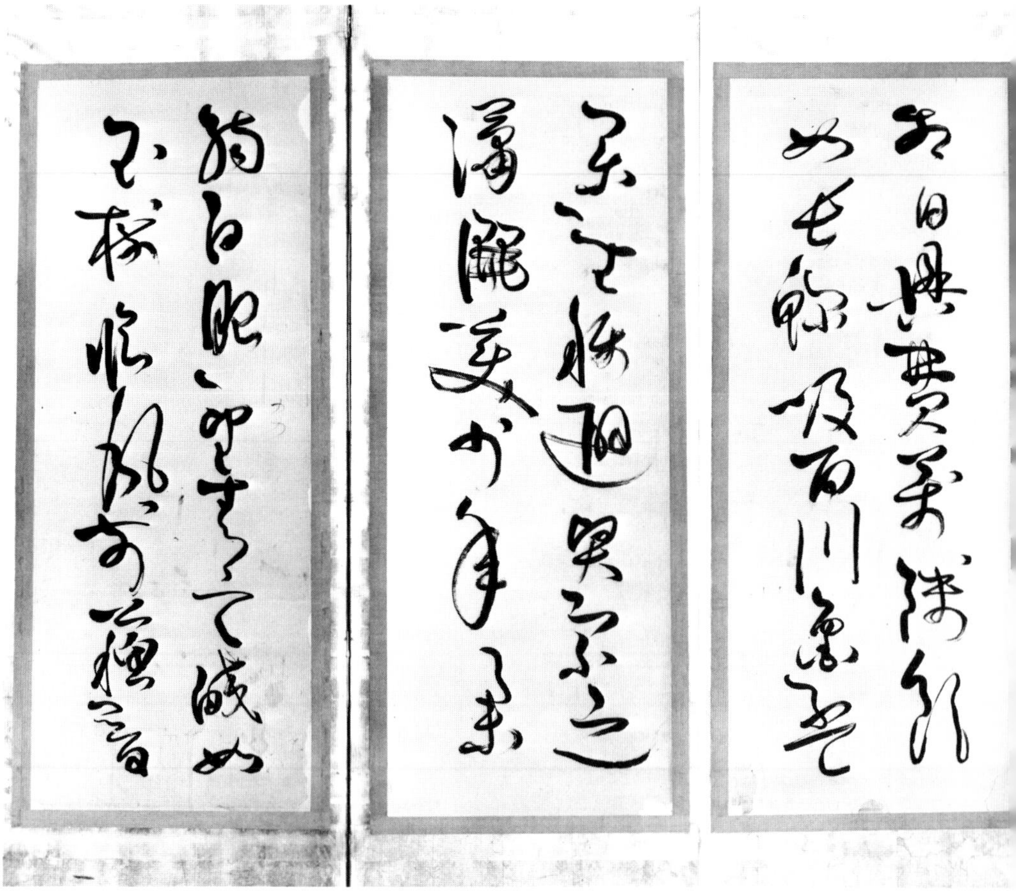

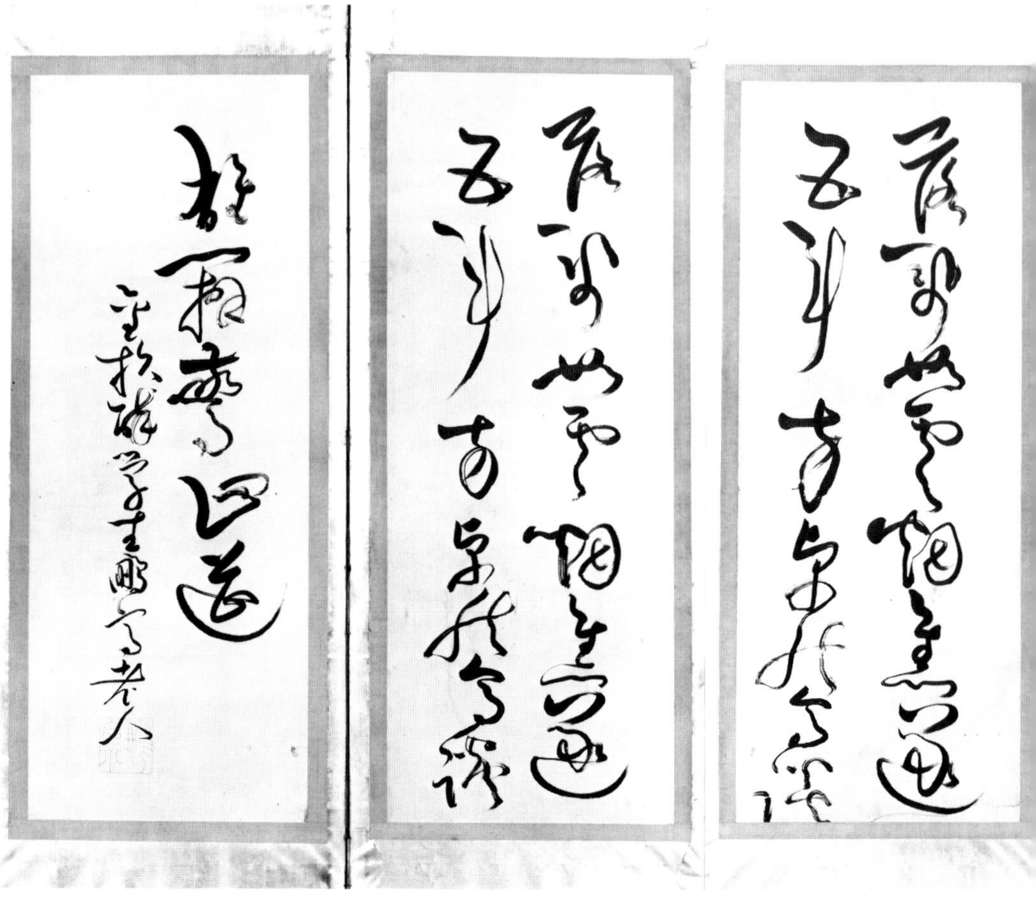

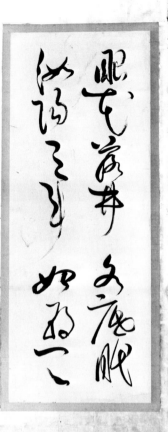

13 Kameda Bōsai, *Eight Immortals of the Wine-cup*

雨霽群峯蒼翠環
湖山風景几間重援
竟何以求其似寫
讀書儀瀾習
丁卯春鷗齋醉寫

14 Kameda Bōsai, *Lake Mountain Scenery*,
1807

the same characters allows us a chance to compare them word for word, and to see where the artist has repeated the same forms and where he has changed them. Thus, we can determine what are the constants in Bōsai's calligraphy at this stage of his life and what are the variables.

The overall composition of the two panels is very similar, although the spacing of the individual characters differs slightly. The bends and tilts to the individual words are surprisingly close, showing that this sense of composition was important to the artist. In the second (left) line of both panels, the first three characters are given a good deal of space, and then the following four words are somewhat cramped together. This allows the second word, *"to"* (forty-five gallons) to float downwards in a semi-circle like a quarter-moon, although with a hook the first time and a more continuous curve the second; the same observations can be made about the following word *"kata"* (direction or manner).

The total aesthetic effect of these screens is that of vigorous motion, with the brushwork barely contained within the large format. Compared with Kinga's calligraphy, it is much more dynamic; compared with that of Shinna, it is more relaxed and full of personal idiosyncrasies. Having learned from both teachers, Bōsai had now developed his own style to the point where it flowed forth with great strength and confidence.

Bōsai continued to develop his landscape painting at this time; two scrolls date from the early months of 1807. The first is a large and somewhat formal work on silk, *Lake Mountain Scenery* (No. 14). Here the mountain peaks are arranged vertically rather than diagonally, giving a sense of stability, but the proportions of the natural and human elements are somewhat fanciful. A fisherman is seen poling past reeds that may recall those of Taiga (see No. 8) as they reach out towards the boat, but the large pavilion in the middleground and the tiny buildings on the plateau both seem disproportionate to the size of the sage walking with his staff in the upper left. Line alternates with wash in the definition of the elements, and visual logic is less vital to the painting than expressive forms and brushwork. Bōsai's poem is important in defining his aims as an artist:

The rain clears, peaks are a rich dark green,
Lake mountain scenery is piled up around my
*   table.*
Picking up my brush, I have no need to seek
*   true resemblance—*
I casually depict my literati and unworldly
*   feelings.*

—Spring of 1807, drunkenly sketched by Bōsai

How seriously we should take the "drunkenly sketched" statement is not clear; the formal arrangement and the brushwork of the painting show care and skill, although the odd proportions suggest that the artist may have been somewhat inebriated at the time. It was a literati jest to imply that the act of painting was based entirely upon the whim of the moment. Artists often claimed to take up the brush while drunk, but in actuality, very few paintings show traces of more than the mild intoxication of the artist.

The second landscape of 1807 (No. 15) bears an inscription by the monk Zentō Kōrō (dates unknown), suggesting that the theme is the Red Cliff:

The Red Cliff is eight thousand feet high,
A rainbow bridge connects two peaks over the
*   river.*
Where is the old immortal Su Shih now?
I know that he has entered the heavens
And is no longer within the confines of the world.
How can one lengthen life by celebrating himself?

Bōsai's signature includes the date of 1807, third month of spring, and he again writes that this is a "drunken sketch." Aside from the charmingly naive row of trees in the upper right, there is nothing untoward about this painting; the composition is balanced between the diagonal rocks and bending trees in the lower left and the tall cliff with a pavilion at the upper right. The sage pausing on the bridge is caught in a moment of stillness, framed in a space cell directly under the vertical cliff. A soft rose color adds vibrancy to the painting, every aspect of which demonstrates Bōsai's confidence in depicting nature in his own idiosyncratic style. His travels no doubt encouraged him to paint landscapes, but his view of nature was not like that of any other artist. He expressed a vision of the world that is both remote and personal, simple but richly flavored, fresh and yet scholarly.

Although his artistic skills were developing now that he no longer was responsible for maintaining a school, Bōsai was not free to journey through Japan as much as he wished. His wife Sae had a recurrence of her illness in 1806, and in the third month of 1807 Bōsai wrote to his friend Yajima that "I had the intention of traveling north, but since last summer my wife has been sick; even at the end of the year, she was unable to get out of bed. This spring her recovery is not yet complete; the infirmities of age seem to be the cause...I have been able to journey briefly with two students to Sekiyado, but I cannot make any longer journeys until my wife is more fully recovered."[17]

In his short trip to Sekiyado (Chiba Prefecture), Bōsai visited Hakoshima Seibi (1758-1815), a retired official who had served the local lord. Seibi asked

14

15

15 Kameda Bōsai, *A Rainbow Bridge*, 1807

Bōsai to give him an art name, and Bōsai chose "Dadako" which means "lazy and indolent." Bōsai explained this odd name by writing:

I must praise Dadako whose nature is neglectful of worldly matters and without restraint. In the spring of 1807 I visited Sekiyado and resided in Hakoshima's house. He is the wealthiest man in the village; his nature is self-indulgent, and he does not worry over household matters. In laziness he already surpasses me. One day he asked me for a name, and I told him "Your character excells over mine, so I will appoint you with this name." He replied that "One should fear such an indolent and lazy person." I said "Your temperament is based upon that of the ancients, exceedingly my own capacity. Therefore I give you a seal reading Dadako, *made of copper, which prints white characters on a red ground."*

Hakoshima Seibi's grandfather had been a pupil of the haiku master Yahantei along with Yosa Buson (1716-1784), and Seibi's father had also been a haiku poet. Bōsai could not have been too far from the mark in the name he banteringly gave his host, since Seibi's own haiku, carved upon his gravestone eight years later, reads:

Nanigoto mo | *No matter what comes,*
hibi yari sutetsu | *every day I do nothing—*
yuki no haru | *snow of the springtime.*

During this visit, Bōsai also repaid the courtesies of the Hakoshima family by writing out a calligraphy plaque for their local temple. However, hearing that his wife's condition had worsened, he quickly returned to Edo. That summer, Sae seems to have recovered sufficiently for Bōsai to visit the resort of Chichibu (Saitama Prefecture). He also went northeast to Tokikawa village to see the Kannon Hall on Tokiyama, also known as Jikōzan after the temple Jikōji. This visit inspired a poem with strong Buddhist connotations from the fifty-five-year-old scholar.

The Kannon Tower on Jikōzan

With my twisted staff, I climb countless layers of rock;
An enchanted castle thrusts up on high, leaning against the steepness.
The rain washes the thousand peaks, green leaves drop down,
In myriad valleys, waterfalls sing to the crumbling rocks.
A sacred voice gushes out from an old Buddha's craggy head,

The cloud of Buddhist law steams inside the cave of a mountain monk.
None of the sweltering heat of the world comes here;
Sitting alone in the pure wind, I am beyond worldly passions.

Bōsai returned that fall to Edo, and at the twelfth month rejoiced at the birth of his first grandchild, a daughter, born to Ryōrai and his wife Ito. This pleasure was soon overcome by the loss of Bōsai's wife on the sixth day of the third month of 1808. He wrote to Yajima:

In the twelfth month I received my first grandchild, a great joy for an old man, but then my wife became more and more ill. Complications developed from the first month, she did not respond to treatment, and finally death came to her. This season is a great darkness to me, and I send this letter in gloom and cheerlessness.

Sae had been known for her kindness, and Bōsai's pupils remembered her fondly in later years.[18]

After his wife's death, there was nothing to keep Bōsai in Edo; to escape his gloom he began to extend his travels. Later in 1808 he journeyed to Sawara to visit the haiku poet Imaizumi Tsunemaru (1751-1810) who had been a friend of Bōsai, Hokuzan and the haiku master Issa (1763-1827) in Edo. In 1792, Tsunemaru had retired to become a lay Buddhist monk and devoted himself to poetry. In his *Tamazasa shū* (Jeweled Bamboo Collection), published in 1812, there is a poem about Bōsai with several puns on his name.

Meeting with Bōsai

You have flown here like a whirlwind ten thousand miles;
Rest your wings, soon you will halt at the Eastern Sea's waters.
Today we meet together in mutual understanding,
And sympathize with the endless travels of the great phoenix.

Bōsai continued to Choshi on the eastern border of Japan, which had previously been visited by a number of poets inspired by its view of the Pacific Ocean. At a gathering of friends, Bōsai wrote about a moon-viewing party on the fifteenth day of the eighth month.

Full autumn: the sea is broad and vast, we cannot see the farther shore.
Over the silent waters, the wind weaves a fine brocade.
Oyster shells glitter temptingly like the Milky Way,

*The waves twinkle with dancing shadows like
    fish or dragons.*
*At the blue sky of the horizon float the huts of
    fishermen,*
*Their homes dipped in the waters under ten
    thousand miles of sky.*
*In this eastern corner of Japan, we have met
    together thirty-five times,*
*And discussed poems about the beautiful lady
    of the moon.*

Bōsai was now famous enough so that when he traveled, people would come to him to ask for poems, paintings or calligraphy. A tea-master friend wrote that Bōsai would be besieged, sometimes until midnight, with requests for his brushwork.[19] Bōsai often collected a fee for writing, but his travels were usually financed in another manner. Wealthy merchants, scholar-officials and landowners of education and taste would often invite painters and poets to their country estates. The artists might stay for days, weeks or even months, enjoying luxuriant surroundings and warm hospitality. In return they would paint, write out poems and inscriptions, give studio names and provide the pleasure of their company. One patron might then offer an introduction to another, and perhaps give the artist some traveling funds. Aside from these small sums, there might be no money involved, but a well-known literatus could travel as long and far as he might wish in this manner.

Bōsai was soon to begin the longest of his journeys, but before leaving he contributed prefaces to several books, including verse collections by various friends as well as volumes of poetry by Su Shih and Yuan Hung-tao. Early in 1809 he also had the sad duty of writing an epitaph for his former pupil, the novelist Takizawa Bakin. That spring he was visited by the monk Ikai (dates unknown), who brought him a painting by Nagamachi Chikuseki (1747-1806), a Nanga artist from Sanuki. Bōsai painted a landscape for Ikai, with an inscription explaining the circumstances (No. 16).

16

*Minami Sanshōki has two waterfalls, the upper
is male and the lower is female. The monk Ikai
brought me Chikuseki's painting of the female
waterfall. Chikuseki had visited Edo and we had
become drinking friends; one year after returning
to his home, he died, and I can't help thinking
of my old comrade. Therefore I have depicted
the male waterfall and given it to Ikai who
brought me Chikuseki's painting.*

—Spring of 1809, Bōsai Kō

16 Kameda Bōsai, *Minami Sanshōki Waterfall*, 1809

Higher in the painting Bōsai wrote a poetic quatrain, utilizing in the third line an image from the T'ang poet Li Po.

I suddenly see a waterfall pouring down the
*   mountain;*
I know that its source is in the sky.
A heavenly being has overturned the Milky Way
And from the clouds spills an endless waterfall.

Perhaps because it was in exchange for a painting by Chikuseki, Bōsai took special care with this landscape. He brushed it on silk, which was rare for him, and added color and more detail than usual. The sage is positioned directly under the waterfall, his wide sleeves crossed behind his back as he contemplates the natural scene. The only trees to be seen are small, and were depicted with the single vertical and multiple horizontal strokes usually utilized by the artist for background vegetation. The absence of larger trees helps focus attention on the figure. Bōsai has added some inner strokes to the mountain forms, and the use of diagonals counterbalances the strong vertical of the waterfall. The soft rich colors and the merging ink-tones at the top of the painting contribute to its rich and subtle effect. Both the inscription and the poem are written in clear regular script within space left open for this purpose, testifying to the artist's careful preparation. Despite the painting's sense of completion, however, the fact that the solitary sage seems to be gazing out beyond the scene adds a sense of mysterious loneliness; this may reflect Bōsai's feelings when thinking of his old friend.

In the fourth month of 1809, Bōsai began a leisurely journey that would last almost three years. His direction was north towards Echigo (Niigata Prefecture) and Sado Island where his friend Yajima Kazue had been preparing for his visit for many months. Bōsai began his travels by boat on the Tonegawa. He stopped at an inn to wait for better weather, writing "A lonely warbler sings in the thousand threads of rain." He then visited Nikko to view the tomb of Tokugawa Ieyasu (1542-1616), the founder of the Tokugawa dynasty.

1809, Summer Fourth Month, an Audience in
*   Nikko's Tōshōgū*

Ending his use of the sacred sword, he rests
*   in his coffin;*
There has been no need to mobilize the army
*   for two hundred years.*
The Shogunate has brought true safety,
And through the land there is the chant "Great
*   Peace."*

During the summer Bōsai sojourned at Sakudaira Namiki's house in Shinshū, where he was entertained by a family that was in the business of producing *sake*. What could be more pleasant for Bōsai? He wrote a poem praising the Namiki's magnificent wine.

Newly cut green bamboo tubes are filled with
*   evening dew,*
It's named *sake* *of the immortals from Mount*
*   Horai.*
The bamboo leaves stir up a delicate fragrance,
Imbibing is like watching the opening
*   of a chrysanthemum's thousand petals.*
In my declining years, my drinking has been
*   somewhat curtailed,*
My withered bowels repeatedly recall my spring-
*   time travels.*
I am haunted by the memory of great thirsts
*   of the past—*
But now I don't envy the immortals a single cup
*   of golden ambrosia!*

When he left to continue his travels, the Namiki family gave him some *sake* to carry with him, and Bōsai shortly thereafter wrote them a letter of heartfelt thanks.

Bōsai traveled onwards, visiting friends and patrons, and made a special visit to the temple of Zenkōji, where an inn had been built for travelers in 1611. This area was famous for its cotton, and at harvest time a large number of merchants gathered at the inn. There were more than two hundred geisha in the region, and various entertainments could be found, ranging from cultural to carnal in spirit. Bōsai stayed here for some time, enjoying the company of his literati friends Kojima Baigai (1722-1841) and Hara Shōshū (1776-1829), both a generation younger than Bōsai. In the autumn, Bōsai went to a nearby mountain to view the full moon.

Watching the Moon at Mount Kyōdai

The clouds pass by, and like opening a box of
*   jewels,*
Pure reflections adorn the region of Mount
*   Kyōdai.*
A thousand paddy fields produce a thousand
*   moons,*
As if all the lunar ladies had come to visit.

There was a calligraphy scroll at the Zenkōji supposed to have been written by the great Sung dynasty master Mi Fu, but when Bōsai examined it, he quickly determined that it was a forgery. In a letter to the Namiki family he complained that the people at Zenkōji were just the type of admire a fake. Nevertheless, he stayed on with his friends, enjoying many painting and poetry parties and nightly visits to the houses of entertainment. Bōsai gave the geisha his calligraphy instead of money, and enjoyed drinking with younger comrades, but he complained that there were no old books in the area. He did, however, meet the reclusive abbot of a nearby temple, and wrote a poem about this unusual monk.

Enjoying-the-Bed Pavilion

The master has a love of horizontal enjoyment,
And is not sought out by the world.
What is the plan of his life?
To stay in bed one hundred years.
He does not see mountains, he does not see
  clouds,
But he has a special refinement.
He is the lord of a tall bed with one pillow,
When visitors come he summons them
  together...
A guest asks: What pleasure is there to always
  stay in bed?
He simply gives a wide-eyed look and does
  not answer.
Resting after drinking, he snores like thunder,
Awakening again, he gathers pearls in a jar.
When drunk, he stays in bed, when sober he
  drinks,
This plan has no flaw.
A single bed, complete enjoyment, aspirations
  ended—
Full pleasure, one bed, there he finds freedom.
Why should he worry about those who can't
  understand him?
Enduring ridicule, he lives on the island of
  longevity...

Although Bōsai felt that most of the people he met at Zenkōji were lacking in refinement, he clearly admired this strange abbot, whose name is not recorded, but who followed the Taoist principle of *wu-wei* (non-action) to the utmost.

Bōsai next journeyed on with Kojima Baigai to Nakano, where Yamada Shōsai (1770-1841) had begun the cultural development of the area by inviting various literati to visit. Shōsai had studied tea and the Chinese seven-string *ch'in*, the musical instrument of sages and poets of the past. Bōsai wrote for him a *Ch'in Record* and a *Ch'in and Calligraphy Tower Record*. Shōsai later published several scholarly books by Bōsai as well as a volume of his own.

On the fifth day of the eighth month, Bōsai and Baigai were guided to the hot springs at Shibu, east of Nakano, by Takanishi Seitan (1774-1822). Bōsai advised Seitan on his poetry, and later wrote a preface when Seitan's verse was published by Yamada Shōsai. Bōsai complimented Seitan as the most talented poet he had met in the Shinshū area. Bōsai also wrote at this time a preface to a book on the poetry of Bashō by Nanimaru, a local haiku master.

Although travel through Japan at this time was primarily on foot, the Namiki family presented Bōsai with a palanquin so that he could be carried over the more difficult mountain passes.

Kashiwabara

The creaking of the bamboo palanquin rides
  on the west wind,
In the sky I see Togakushi peak.
Rain strikes the bamboo screen, suddenly
  darkening the mountain;
At the gate of the grotto there are white clouds
  like chains.

Kashiwabara was the home of the haiku poet Issa, whom Bōsai had met at a party in Edo in 1804. Bōsai did not linger there, however, but continued on to Takada, where he became ill. The "Double Nines" festival, the ninth day of the ninth month, was a time for scholars and poets to admire chrysanthemums, climb high peaks and compose poetry, but Bōsai could not even enjoy the sight of girls carrying dogwood branches to ward off evil spirits.

Sick in Bed in Takada During the Double Nines Festival

Among the lonely autumn colors, my spirit
  grieves
As I lie sick in bed in this corner of the
  northern sea.
The wind in the trees turns my thoughts to
  returning home,
The Double Nines festival increases my feelings
  of nostalgia.
Already I can see snow falling on the
  mountain peaks
And I hear the mournful cry of wild geese over
  the ocean.
Under the cold sky, maple leaves fall before they
  turn color,
The chrysanthemums in the cold earth refuse
  to open their petals.
I don't feel comfortable with local customs,
It is with acquaintances, not friends, that I tip
  a cup of wine.
For medicine, the dogwood is enough,
From my pillow I listen in vain to footsteps
  climbing the tower.
In my home, under the hedges the flowers are
  blooming—
To the east, the mountains are buried in white
  clouds.

Despite this melancholy moment, Bōsai soon recovered his health and continued his northern journey. He passed the sand dunes at Nachizaki, reminding him of the legend of a "foolish lord" who tried to move mountains.

The sea wind has the strength to shift mountains,
After seeing level plains, the sand dunes seem
   like great peaks.
Last year I climbed mountains, this year not—
But I have to laugh at those
   who waste their strength trying to move them.

Bōsai continued on to Kashiwazaki, where several friends offered him hospitality; he now had more patrons than he needed. Moving onwards to Izumo-zaki, Bōsai visited the family of the Zen monk and poet Ryōkan (1757-1831). The monk's father Samon had preferred poetry to business, and since Ryōkan decided to take the tonsure, a younger brother was now the head of the family.

At first it appears that Bōsai met only the relatives of Ryōkan; in a thank-you letter he mentions that he appreciated the gift of a fish, that he had contracted a skin disease from eating badger meat, and that he sends his greetings to Ryōkan. Later the two met a number of times, and various stories exist about their friendship. The most famous account tells how Ryōkan forgot his guest while viewing the moon; this anecdote is given in the Introduction. Another time, according to legend, Bōsai went to meet Ryōkan at his Gogō-an hermitage and found the monk doing *zazen* (Zen meditation). Bōsai waited serenely for half a day before the monk noticed he was there, then they had a good talk. In a third story, Bōsai was giving a lecture when Ryōkan and his pupils arrived. They were dressed so poorly that they were not allowed into the hall, and Bōsai had to follow them and try to persuade them to return.[20]

A more reliable story relates to the calligraphy of the two masters. Bōsai had been invited to write two large banners for a Shintō festival, and the cloth was being prepared when Ryōkan came to visit. Bōsai invited Ryōkan to write in his stead, so the monk took up the brush and wrote "Hachiman-sama" (the name of a Shintō deity) in the native *kana* script, akin to an alphabet. Bōsai was surprised, as he had been planning to use the more formal and elegant Chinese characters. Ryōkan then wrote "Gosairei" ("Shintō Festival") on the second banner, and Bōsai clapped his hands in delight.[21] There are two main points to this story. The first is that Ryōkan sometimes wrote in the simplest kind of script, so that anyone might easily read it. The second is that Bōsai had great respect for Ryōkan and his calligraphy.

Ryōkan composed a series of four short poems about men that he admired. One of these was Bōsai, who appears in the following quatrain from the *Yūkai yonshu* (Four Poems about Friends).[22]

Bōsai is a wise man who does not fuss about
   worldly matters;
For some reason he has come to this town.
Yesterday, in the thronged streets,
I saw him laughing as someone supported him
   by the arm.[23]

Bōsai also wrote a poem about Ryōkan, modestly suggesting that he did not share the monk's enlightenment.

Presented to the Zen Monk Ryōkan

I envy your transcendence:
   You are not like other monks.
With <u>sake</u> cups filled to the brim,
   We talk and laugh by the Buddhist altar lights.
You travel here and there,
   but your heart does not cling,
Unlike most men who are
   possessed by things of the world.
I am unworthy to climb with you
   the five sacred mountains,
It is too late for me to hope for nirvana.

The different personalities of Bōsai and Ryōkan show up clearly in their calligraphy. Both have individual and free styles, and both were influenced by the "wild cursive" script of the T'ang dynasty monk Huai-su. However, Ryōkan's writing has the qualities of simplicity and inner strength that relate directly to his Zen training. In 1920, one of Ryōkan's haiku poems in his distinctive calligraphy was carved onto a stone which was erected next to his hermitage the Gogō-an, high in the mountains of the Niigata area (No. 17).[24]

Taku hodo wa	*Enough for a fire—*
kaze ga motte kuru	*the soft breeze has carried here*
ochiba kana	*autumn's fallen leaves*

The monk here utilized Chinese characters purely for their sounds, writing in a complex form of script that is now known as *man'yōgana*. The characters themselves, however, were brushed with an affecting simplicity. The gently modulated lines are usually thin, and the spaces left between them give a feeling of astringent loneliness. One can sense the personal modesty and self-effacement of Ryōkan; his depth of scholarship and skill as a calligrapher are both subordinated to the humble expression of a monk who called himself a "great fool."[25]

Ryōkan's calligraphy, despite its terseness, is extremely fluent. Bōsai's writing, in contrast, is more fully developed and outwardly expressive, with a great deal of internal tension and release. Since most stories about Bōsai and Ryōkan come from the monk's followers in the Niigata area, they tend to emphasize Ryōkan's importance in the relationship, but there

17

17 Sō Ryōkan, *Enough for a Fire*

is no doubt that the two poet-calligraphers became close friends, and that Bōsai's cursive script did gain in fluency of brush movement from this time onwards. After he returned to Edo, a *senryū* was circulated:

Bōsai wa	*Now that Bōsai*
Echigo ga heride	*has visited Echigo,*
ji ga kuneri	*his writing twists and turns!*[26]

If this was the influence of Ryōkan, it shows that the two artists shared something in character as well as in calligraphy. The freedom of spirit that Bōsai gained in his travels, brought forth by the opportunity to please his friends by writing out poems, certainly affected his art and led him to manifestations of a spirit that was no longer tied to worldly ambitions.

On the twenty-fourth day of the twelfth month of 1809 (which would have been early in 1810 by our calendar), Bōsai reached the city of Niigata, where he celebrated the New Year. He also visited his pupil Nakamura Kyū'emon (dates unknown) in Suibara, and shortly thereafter wrote him a letter which contains Bōsai's views on becoming a scholar.

The Way of scholarship is based primarily upon reading. It doesn't matter whether you study classics or history first; men of old read the classics at dawn, history in the afternoons and poetry in the evenings. When reading becomes natural to you, your understanding will flower. If you have a good teacher, the work of one year can be accomplished in half a year; if you use your full energy for learning, nothing is impossible. After two or three years of hard work, little by little you will understand more and more through repeated reading. If you continue to use your full energy, a thawing will take place, and what seemed difficult will become easy.

Judging from this letter, Bōsai followed the traditional views that one must study first, and comprehension would come gradually. He emphasized the importance of a good teacher, but felt it was ultimately the devotion of a student to his books that would produce a true scholar.

While in Niigata, Bōsai seems to have had a love affair with a geisha named Tomiji. He wrote one of his rare poems in Japanese *kana* script for her, with an introduction:

In Niigata, the geisha Tomiji is so beautiful that I send her this poem:

Sugi sarishi	*In a previous*
saki ni sadameshi	*existence, our fate was set*
enishi nareba	*because of karma—*
nado itowameya	*if people speak ill of me*
tame ni tatsu nawa	*[when I'm with you] I don't care*

Bōsai, visiting the entertainment district, would climb to a second-storey room to admire the view of the sea while drinking with Tomiji. He was waiting for the snow to melt so he could cross to Sado Island, but in the company of the beautiful geisha, he must have enjoyed the long pause in his travels. He also visited the painter Ishikawa Kansai (dates unknown), and inscribed one of his landscapes with a poem. Kansai did not have much success as an artist; he wore a threadbare old black kimono and was supported by his wife. Paying little attention to his putative profession as a shipping agent, Kansai enjoyed painting in literati style; the encouragement of Bōsai must have been a boon to his spirit.

In early spring Bōsai made a short trip to Matsuno, where he wrote out a calligraphy plaque "Camelia Pavilion" for a patron with a garden containing "one great tree, in which the flowers open every spring like a burning fire." Bōsai continued on to Iwase, where he wrote a poem celebrating a garden with a magnificent pair of pine trees. He presented the poem to his host, utilizing regular script, perhaps for the sake of comprehension. The writing is forceful and vigorous; it is primarily angular in style with occasional curving strokes for contrast (No. 18).

18

On the Pair of Pines in the Garden of Tanahashi Bokumin at Iwase in Hoku-etsu

Your ancestors planted pine trees a few inches high:
Did they realize that today they would become a pair of dragons?
Frosty trunks and snowy branches are firmly rooted below;
Green whiskers and black colors stand proud throughout the winter.
Auspicious mist, together they encage the miles-high moon;
Their pure music wafts on high to harmonize with heaven's wind.
Twisting branches look like dragons fighting for the magic jewel;
The dense greenery of their needles is like the shaking of long manes.
One might take them for arching whales slapping the vast sea,
Or watch, amazed, as they clutch at clouds rising to the azure sky.
Mulberry fields and oceans: how many times have they turned into each other?[27]
But your house, Sir, will surely endure as long as these trees themselves,

Generation after generation,
  carrying on your ancestor's enterprise,
Forever together with this pair of pines, lasting
  without end.[28]

—*The seventh year of Bunka, 1810, the second month of spring, written by old man Bōsai Kō*

This praise of his pines, including a wish for longevity, must have greatly pleased the educated merchant Tanahashi. This was exactly the kind of work that was appropriate for a wandering literatus to brush for a generous host.

Bōsai finally reached Izumozaki, where there were boats which sailed to Sado Island. Before embarking, however, he painted several works and wrote out poems for local patrons. Most interesting of these are four panels still extant with ink paintings of bamboo, orchids, chrysanthemums and plum blossoms (figure 2), the "four gentlemen." These subjects each have symbolic overtones in representing the virtuous scholar, who can bend without breaking (bamboo), does not show off his elegance (the Chinese orchid), blooms late in life (the chrysanthemum) and is not afraid to come forth in difficult times (the plum, which blossoms at the end of winter). These "gentlemen" subjects were often favored by literati, because they afforded opportunities for the free expression of one's spirit through ink-play and calligraphic brushwork. Bōsai, unlike most scholar-painters, rarely attempted these subjects, so these panels of 1810 are especially notable.

Waiting for a boat to Sado Island, Bōsai was surprised to meet a monk from Sendai he had known three decades earlier, when they were both studying Confucianism.

A Chance Meeting with Sendai's Sekiryō Oshō at Hoku-etsu Umpo

Thirty years have gone by in one snap of the
  fingers,
I am ashamed of my white hair, living in the
  dusty world.
We meet at Izumozaki, but there is nothing
  I can say—
I smile and point out the window to a stretch
  of mountains.

After a month at Izumozaki, Bōsai crossed the sea, a distance of about eighteen miles, to Sado Island. Sailing on an eastern wind, the journey took about six hours. Bōsai wrote a set of three quatrains about his journeys, the last of which may refer to the voyage to Sado Island.

18 Kameda Bōsai, *The Pair of Pines*, 1810

48

Three Poems on the Northern Crossing

Long shoreline, wide beach, vastness without end,
The blue sky is immersed in countless miles of
waves and billows.
In the distance, the ocean and sky reach to the
northern peoples—
The autumn wind descends on a stone arrowhead
from a far-off time.
Mountains face the sea with rice paddies
between them;
I proceed from village to village to the sound
of the harvest.
In my later years, I like wine and despise riches—
I can even enjoy the bone-chilling wind as I
travel onwards.
The wind on the Japan Sea smells of fish, rain
falls abundantly,
Several angry dragons are coiled over the waves.
In an instant the clouds rise up, a moment
later they settle—
Half the sky alternates from black to white.

On Sado Island Bōsai finally met with his friend Yajima Kazue. As gold had been found in the area, Yajima decided to erect a lecture hall and was considering the establishment of a Confucian academy. Bōsai was consulted, and named the hall "Reifūkan" (Inspiring Wind Hall). Although the plans were never fully realized, in one building on Yajima's estate a portrait of Confucius was installed; Bōsai wrote out a poem that was carved into an ornamental log suspended on bamboo, calling himself "just a loafer whose brush follows the law of the waves."[29] Bōsai lectured at the Reifūkan on the *Spring and Autumn Annals,* and also gave a talk on the Confucian *Analects* at Aikawa, another educational center on Sado Island. He wrote in a letter "This is a place where the crossing brings people together; fifty or sixty gather to hear my lectures, which are presented in a temple." Bōsai also visited the local scholars, finding only Honma Mokusai (1755-1829) truly worthy. Bōsai later commented that Sado Island had "one and a half scholars." Mokusai was the one, and the others all together equalled a half.[30] Mokusai, who was also a lover of *sake,* received a calligraphy plaque from Bōsai reading "Retirement Hall of Small Fame," a modest title for his hermitage.

Traveling about the island, Bōsai reached the temple of Rengehōji, where at the request of the abbot Kankai (1747-1822) he wrote out a large signboard for the main hall. Later Bōsai was to send Kankai a text celebrating the abbot's success in obtaining a full set of Buddhist scriptures for the temple; this text was carved in stone and still remains on the grounds of Rengehōji.

Despite all this activity, Bōsai does not seem to have been very happy on Sado Island. He wrote in a letter that "The smoky island is very lonely, the boundless waves are only white flutterings in the vastness....I long to see Hara Shōshū in Kashiwazaki. Please give my best regards to all my friends, I will try to return next month."

Bōsai did in fact return to Kashiwazaki after a stay of three months on Sado Island. He now took some time to relax, enjoying drinking with his friend Hara Shōshū in the entertainment district. One evening Shōshū painted an ink portrait of an *Oiran* (high-class geisha) and Bōsai added a *senryū* suggesting that the penniless scholars were worth no more to a geisha than a sliver of moon to lovers of nature.

Bakarashi	*How foolish it is*
ogamin su ni to	*to bow and worship to the*
mikka no tsuki	*third-day crescent moon*

When the time came to part with Shōshū, Bōsai wrote a melancholy poem in his more familiar Chinese style.

Farewell to Shōshū

Drifting aimlessly like sagebrush,
I unexpectedly met you at a lonely temple.
With a crazy dance, we talk freely as our fancy
takes us,

Figure 2 Kameda Bōsai,
Plum Blossoms, 1810,
Kato Collection,
Izumozaki

Singing sad songs, we come to a strong affection.
Drunk, we both dream of the moon and
 mountains of our homes,
Stopping at an inn, we are surprised by the
 wintry wind.
It's hard to realize that our friendship faces a
 lifetime separation:
The black-haired youth and the white-haired
 old man.

Shōshū, an aspiring scholar of some excellence, determined to travel to Edo, but when he arrived he was quite ill and had to remain in bed for several months. He was assisted by Bōsai's pupil Maki Ryōkō; one friend who visited reported that if there were questions of scholarship, they would ask Shōshū, who would give the correct answers from his bed. After recovering his health, he left Edo in the following year; gathered together for the farewell party at Ryōkō's house were many of Bōsai's friends including Tachi Ryū-an and Kojima Baigai.

Bōsai was also determined to return to Edo. A new house had been prepared for him in Kanasugi, and Ryōrai had also built a house in the same region. Bōsai, however, was still busy with commissions from patrons and friends in the Niigata area. He wrote out the *Heart Sutra* for a patron whose father who had recently died; this is one of the few examples of Bōsai writing a Buddhist text. A geisha in Tsubame named Ō-ume, who was kind-hearted but not beautiful, tried to make Bōsai forget Tomiji, but without success. Bōsai still cared for Tomiji so much that he wrote a poem in the Chinese *tzu* (song) form, making many elegant comparisons between the geisha and the beauty of plum blossoms and the graceful form of the willow. He ended the poem with an expression of his distress at their separation.

Bōsai spent the New Year in Tsubame, where by Japanese count he celebrated his sixtieth birthday. He had long since felt free of any burdensome restrictions, but he could not help but reflect upon his life at this juncture.

Written on New Year's Morning in Hoku-etsu

Traveling for three years,
 now I arrive here;
Twice I have met the springtime
 at the shores of the North Sea.
A wild goose severs the evening snow
 on the peaks of Echigo,
The Shinano River is frozen over,
 fish lie deeply submerged.
This wandering old man
 is ashamed of his sixty years;
Who can sympathize with his spirit,
 traveling ten thousand miles on the road?

Stopping at an inn,
 I open the New Year's wine,
By the clear window,
 I wipe the glistening from my eyes.

Bōsai's spirit was invigorated, however, by the knowledge of his freedom, as another poem of the same time makes clear.

Lofty, lofty, happiness at sixty years—
No official position, no salary, I can do what
 I wish.
Leisurely I sip wine, leisurely become drunk,
My reality is the peacefulness of a man who
 owns nothing.

One reason Bōsai may have delayed his return to Edo was the bitter cold; that year in Echigo the snow reached a height of almost five feet, and the freezing temperatures continued well into the spring. Bōsai wrote a letter to Yajima Kazue in Sado Island on the twentieth day of the second month, saying in part:

Last year I had intended to return to my home, but I have remained in Tsubame....there has been an immense snow this spring, snow has piled up until it covers the eaves of the houses. It remains very cold, so I do not get up from the kotatsu *(heater), but shrink my head down to keep warm....When the weather improves I will set out for Edo....My thanks for your hospitality and please give my greetings to everyone....I would like to send you a soft-shell turtle, but they have not appeared since last spring; deer have also become rare, and the ocean is too rough to be fished, so I only drink wine.*

During the winter in northern Japan, people were accustomed to freezing temperatures that were rare in Edo, and Bōsai was surprised to see how sleighs with sails skated over the frozen sea.

Composed on a Winter Day in Hoku-etsu

For half a year, not one point of blue in the sky;
Clouds fill the heavens, snow blocks the roads,
Mountains and rivers are buried, one cannot
 see their borders,
Villages are deeply embedded under the arctic
 lights.
Icicles like jade blinds hang outside in the wind,
Sleighs sail over the frozen sea.
I have been here three years,
 but have not become accustomed to Echigo,
Yet I cannot doubt that the sleighs
 move easily when thrust by the wind.

Bōsai's chief patrons in Tsubame were Jimbo Ryūha and his son Kyōson. When Bōsai departed, he composed a poem of appreciation for their kind hospitality, which had eased his journeys and helped prevent loneliness.

Given in Farewell to Jimbo

I have wandered for three years as a guest of the road,
For sixty years a willful character like men of old.
The master here loves me, and is not stingy with money;
I have found his home agreeable for my self-indulgent tastes.
He has <u>sake</u> like a river, and meat like a mountain,
One day, once drunk; one hundred days, one hundred times drunk;
In this manner for three years I have frequently come here.
When you wave, I recognize your house for my home,
Forgetting the sadness of travel, forgetting my poverty,
I know I can return to your house and thus feel satisfied.
This morning, it's time to separate, we have a farewell drink—
Only now do I realize that for three years I have been a guest.

Bōsai's large calligraphy of this poem is still in the collection of the Jimbo family in Tsubame.

Bōsai slowly made his way back to Edo, stopping to visit friends he had met on his outward journey and writing various poems and inscriptions. One of the most interesting people that he revisited was the doctor Harada Jakusai (dates unknown), known as the "plum tree thief." Bōsai had previously written a poem about Jakusai's most famous (or infamous) exploit:

Presented to the Plum Thief, Old Man Jakusai

Old man Jakusai has a wonderful peculiarity,
This strange habit concerns plum blossoms.
He so loves the plum, he does not notice people,
And has no need for a home in the deep mountains or shaded valleys.
The Kugamiyama temple had one tree, so fine
That when it blossomed it had no match in the entire country.
Jakusai took one look and went mad; he returned that evening,
Carrying a spade, traveling in disguise to transplant it.
All the monks, when the thief arrived,
Took out clubs and sticks and made a clamor, striking the bell;

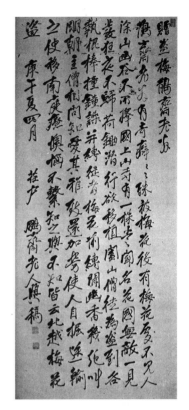

Figure 3 Kameda Bōsai, *Presented to the Plum Thief, Old Man Jakusai*, Harada Collection, Nakajima, Niigata

They captured the thief in front of the plum tree.
The monks were surprised to find you, a man of refinement.
The next morning, the chief monks discussed the matter.
Admiring your elegance, they decided to give you the tree.
They sent a messenger to transport the plum
To your southern garden, and thus healed your troubled spirit.
Not knowing the full story,
Everyone calls you the plum thief of Hoku-etsu.

Bōsai's calligraphy of this poem in regular script (figure 3) is preserved in a small exhibition hall in the Harada mansion, which also boasts a fine old tea-house utilized by Ryōkan.[31]

Bōsai visited other literati patrons on his journey, and in particular spent a good deal of time with his artist friend Kushiro Unsen (1759-1811). After studying painting in Nagasaki where he had access to Chinese works, Unsen had lived in the Kansai (Kyoto and Osaka) region for some time. He then moved to Edo for a short while, and traveled onwards to Niigata. Divorcing his wife Mitsu, Unsen settled down with a woman from the Echigo area, where he became famous as a local painter. He combined a rich knowledge of literati traditions with a creative intelligence often fortified by the drinking of *sake*. His finest paintings have an extraordinary power of conception, along

with freely applied brushstrokes showing his skill in the Nanga tradition. Although some of his works are conservative in style, he was capable of the dynamic forcefulness that can be seen in *Viewing a Waterfall* (No. 19). Like Bōsai's painting on silk (see No. 16), Unsen depicted a sage directly under the waterfall, metaphysically receiving its flow which is represented in the painting by emptiness.[32] Rocks, trees and mountains seem to lean towards the waterfall, but they shy away from its force.

Compared with Bōsai, Unsen was more thoroughly trained in Nanga painting, and his brushwork is at times more sophisticated. Both artists, however, expressed their own spirit through depictions of natural scenes. Bōsai developed a more characteristic style, while Unsen showed more variety of approach and a greater range of subject matter. Considering their love of painting, poetry and wine, it is not surprising that the two should become close friends.[33]

The two artists went to Shinnogawa to visit Yamaya Sakai, who had a garden with a famous stone. Unsen painted a literati work for the family, while Bōsai wrote the *Sekisui shoki* (Record of the Villa of Layered Greenery). Hearing that the sound of spring water upon the famous stone made a chanting sound in the garden, Bōsai composed an eight-line poem celebrating nature.

> *Echi Mountain's stone*
> *Was not polished and was not shined.*
> *Its design was created by a flowing stream,*
> *The texture came from the circling waves.*
> *People ask "Was it made by a devil or a god?"—*
> *When I see this skill,*
> *I know it was not a devil or a god,*
> *But the workmanship of nature.*

Bōsai and Unsen became extremely close friends, but in the fourth month it was finally time for Bōsai to depart, and they bade each other a final farewell.

Farewell to Kushiro Unsen

> *Our parting was hurried,*
> *But nevertheless full of deep feelings.*
> *It is difficult for old men's eyes to endure:*
> *Together we wept over our different journeys.*

> *I traveled through Hoku-etsu for three years;*
> *during that time we met and parted many times.*
> *Meeting was always a joy, and parting was always a great sorrow. The day I finally returned to the east, he walked a long way to see me off. The weeping and lamentation of our parting*

19

19 Kushiro Unsen, *Viewing a Waterfall*

moved nearby people to tears; the deep emotions that sincerely came forth could be understood by everyone.

Half a year later, Unsen was eating noodles in a *soba* shop in Izumozaki when he suddenly suffered a heart attack and died almost immediately; he was fifty-two years old. When Bōsai heard the news he was shocked, and wrote a long epitaph for Unsen which records his admiration and his grief.[34]

Bōsai's return to Edo was certainly leisurely; the entire journey took eight months. He paused in Ōimura, where he composed a quatrain:

Suddenly I see a waterfall hanging through a
* screen of greenery,*
Its source must be in the heavens.
The creator's hands have hollowed it from the
* Milky Way;*
Its pouring causes the dusty world to wash its face.

Bōsai wrote to the Jimbo family that since walking was difficult for him in the summer heat, he stopped at the hot springs in Shinshū where he was generously treated. In Suzaka, he visited Komazawa Seisen (1737-1818), who had been the economic advisor for the local *daimyō*, but was particularly fond of the seven-string Chinese *ch'in*. Seisen had been a pupil of Nakae Tochō (also known as Shōka, 1748-1816), a "master of the five arts" including poetry, music, calligraphy, painting and seal-carving; Tochō had helped Seisen acquire an old Chinese *ch'in*. Bōsai wrote a *Kokinki* (Ancient *Ch'in* Record) for Seisen, referring obliquely to the famous Chinese *ch'in* pieces "Tall Mountains" and "Flowing Waters" as well as more directly to "The Shaded Valley Stream" which was one of twenty-four landscape songs set to texts by the T'ang dynasty poet Li Po.

The Record of an Old Ch'in Owned by Sawa Seisen

In this house there is an old ch'in *made in China, where it gave pleasure to men of ancient times. In the summer of 1811 I traveled to Shinshū and visited Seisen, and was able to see his treasured instrument. Its form is graceful, and it has a fine old pale lacquer that has crackled over the years. Several centuries old, it is truly an extraordinary object. When the tuning pegs are turned and the strings are pressed near the studs, they resound as clear and pure as a precious stone. The sound is like the harmony of snow and bamboo, or of the wind entering the pines. Brought over the ocean, this is one of the rare such* ch'ins *in Japan. As I had never seen an instrument of such wondrous antiquity, I requested that the master play me a piece on this* ch'in. *He took me up to a tower which*

faced the tall mountains and commanded a pure view of the flowing waters. The master wore a feathered robe and a gauze cap, and lit fragrant incense. He performed "The Shaded Valley Stream," and the sound was like the wind in the pines, or like the rustling of bamboo in the breeze. Along with the tall mountains and flowing waters it reverberated harmoniously.[35]

It was through the kindness of his other music-loving patron, Yamada Shōsai, that Bōsai was given a *ch'in* of his own (No. 20). An instrument with an extraordinary deep red lacquer finish was built for him, with an inscription hidden within it: "Constructed for Bōsai Sensei by his pupil Yamada [Bun]sei in Shinshū, 1811." Perhaps it was modeled upon an ancient Chinese instrument, but the dark red tone of the lacquer is unique, and the *ch'in* is a rare example of a Japanese instrument of the period. How well Bōsai could play the *ch'in* is unknown, but even if he could only strum a simple tune or two, like every scholar he would have appreciated the instrument as a means of harmonizing his mind and communicating with past literati masters.[36]

In the autumn, Bōsai visited the Namiki family in Sakudaira, and there he celebrated his actual birthday, becoming sixty by Japanese count. A banquet was held in his honor, and he became quite drunk, composing poems freely without his usual technical skill.

Aimlessly wandering like a lunatic, I was clumsy
* from birth,*
Now sixty years have disappeared day by day,
* month by month.*
Relying on your kindness for a party, I've
* become so drunk—*
I don't even know how old I am!

As he neared Edo, Bōsai must have wondered how well he would like returning to live in the city. On one hand, he no doubt missed his friends and family, and was weary of travel; on the other hand, he had enjoyed traveling by the mountains and seas, and now he must settle down to a more circumscribed life. Pausing at a patron's house in the tenth month, Bōsai painted a horizontal landscape on silk (No. 21). Jutting rocks in the foreground are offset by more placid mountains in the distance; a sage crosses a bridge in the lower left, but there is no way for him to join his friends conversing in a lake-side hut on the right. The mood is peaceful and serene, but Bōsai's poem shows his ironic mood.

Harmony comes from living in the mountain
* forest,*
Misery comes from living in the capital.

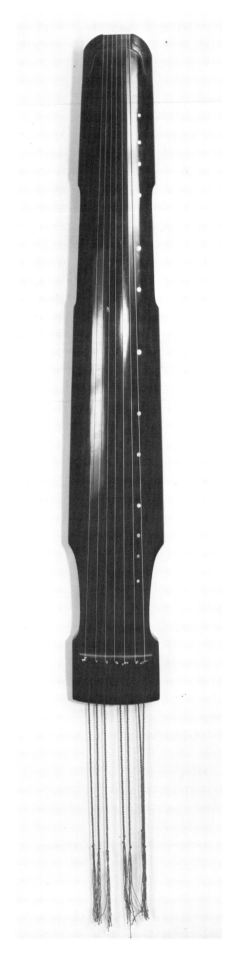

Is this true or not?
With a smile, I inscribe this painting.

In the upper right-hand corner, Bōsai added:

—Bunka 1811, tenth month, playfully
painted by the fisherman of the ink river.[37]

Bōsai finally reached Edo on the eleventh day of the twelfth month (already 1812 by the Western calendar). He had been gone for two years and eight months. During that time he had significantly enlarged his artistic world; not only had he made many new friends and seen the nature of the Niigata region in all seasons, he had also established himself as an artist as well as scholar. The admiration that he received from his hosts and other friends was balanced by the deepening of his spirit through a sense of union with nature. His world was now that of the countryside as well as the city, and the confidence with which he practiced the arts of poetry, calligraphy and painting demonstrates his mastery of all aspects of the literati tradition.

1   In a preface Bōsai wrote later for one of Ichidō's more than thirty published books, he recalled that when Ichidō and Ryōrai were both struggling to memorize the classics, they wished merely to become farmers.

2   Kien was a follower of the Chu Hsi school, but had a tolerant attitude towards other forms of Confucianism.

3   He then collected colophons from famous scholars over the next thirty years. See Miyeko Murase, *Japanese Art: Selections from the Mary and Jackson Burke Collection*, (New York, 1975), pp. 243-248.

4   The Sung dynasty poet and patriot Hsieh Ao met his friends every evening at the time when the tide was high, an example of steadfast loyalty.

5   While at a painting and calligraphy party in Kyoto, Bōsai inscribed a landscape by Kien with an intriguing quatrain:

A jeweled dish and gallons of ink,
A well-soaked brush and time for enjoyment—
With wine as ink, the pleasure never ceases,
Bringing forth the mountains in my heart.

The phrase "mountains in my heart" later became the title for Bōsai's woodblock book of landscape designs (see No. 28).

6   The old fort had been destroyed in 1580, and its remnants became a testimonial to the vanity of human ambitions and to the unyielding strength of nature.

7   A number of scrolls by Hōitsu bear inscriptions by Bōsai (see Nos. 42, 45 and 54).

8   This would already have become 1804 in the Western calendar.

9   These were known in Japan through woodblock books and the works of the visiting artist I Fu-chiu (who came to Nagasaki several times in the early eighteenth century). That Bōsai knew the works of I Fu-chiu is proven by Bōsai's box inscription for a landscape by the Chinese master that is now in the Mitchell Hutchinson Collection. Bōsai's landscapes, like those of his teacher Kinga, are quite close in spirit and technique to those of I Fu-chiu.

10 The scroll is not dated, but the style suggests that it is a relatively early work. The two seals below the signature are also found on dated examples of 1802-1805; see Appendix B. This is also one of the rare scrolls not signed "Bōsai" but rather "Written by Kameda Kō."

20 *Seven-String Ch'in Presented to Bōsai*, 1811

21 Kameda Bōsai, *Living in the Mountain Forest*, 1811

11 Chuang Tzu had suggested "once you have the meaning you do not need the words."

12 Husbands and wives traveling together were known as "camels."

13 The stone still remains at the spot, with the roots of a maple tree growing in its cracks.

14 In the *Pen-ts'ao kang-mu* (Herb Chronical) by Li Shih-chen of the Ming dynasty, lotus root juice is listed as a good tonic for "blood disease," and could also help relieve the thirst caused by drinking too much alcohol.

15 For example, he inscribed another portrait of Su Shih by Tani Bunchō that year.

16 See Jonathan Chaves, *Pilgrim of the Clouds* (New York and Tokyo, 1978) for an essay and translations of Yuan's poems.

17 Sae's illness particularly affected her stomach; Yajima sent arrowroot powder from Sado Island as medicine. For the texts to many of Bōsai's letters, see Yamamoto Shūnosuke, "Kameda Bōsai no Sado jin'en shokan" (Kameda Bōsai's Letters to Friends on Sado Island), *Sado shigaku*, Nos. 1-4, 7 (Sado, 1959-71) and the same author's "Kameda Bōsai no Echigo jin'en shokan" (Kameda Bōsai's Letters to Friends in Echigo), *Echisa kenkyū*, No. 29 (Niigata, 1970).

18 In Mori Ōgai's historical novel *Hōjō Katei*, Sae is praised for her kindness towards Bōsai's students.

19 From Tagawaya Kōtarō, *Kandan sūkoku* (Several Hours of Quiet Conversation), quoted in Sugimura, op. cit., p. 81.

20 These stories are given in Harada Kampei, "Bōsai to Ryōkan" (Bōsai and Ryōkan), *Bokubi*, Vol. 148 (1965), p. 32. See also Yamamoto Shūnosuke, *Kameda Bōsai shōden* (A Short Biography of Kameda Bōsai, Niigata, 1951), pp. 20-25.

21 Ibid, and also quoted in Sugimura, op. cit., p. 114.

22 The original Ryōkan manuscript is reproduced in *Bokubi*, Vol. 213 (1971), p. 15.

23 Apparently Bōsai, somewhat tipsy, was being helped down the street. Perhaps this was during the Shintō festival for which the banners had been written.

24 Through the kindness of the current monk of the Gogō-an, Shibuya Keia (himself an enthusiast of Ryōkan's calligraphy), I was allowed to make a rubbing of this stone for display in the current exhibition.

25 For further translations of Ryōkan's poetry, see John Stevens, *One Robe, One Bowl: The Zen Poetry of Ryōkan* (New York and Tokyo, 1977) and Burton Watson, *Ryōkan: Zen Monk-Poet of Japan* (New York, 1977).

26 See Togari Shoshin'an, "Ryōkan no sho to Bōsai shoshite kaiso" (Ryōkan's Calligraphy and Bōsai: Expressions of the Heart), *Atorie*, Vol. 15, No. 8 (June, 1938), p. 18.

27 Referring to the myth of the mulberry field which after aeons of time turns into an ocean, and after more aeons turns back into a mulberry field.

28 Translation by Jonathan Chaves.

29 In 1951, a memorial hall was constructed which contains Bōsai's inkstone and brush-holder, souvenirs of his visit well over a century earlier.

30 See Yamamoto, op. cit., p. 25.

31 The "plum thief" was so well known in the area that Ryōkan and others also wrote poems about his exploit.

32 This suggests the purification ritual of Shugendō, a religion of mountain ascetics.

33 See Furukawa Osamu, "Kameda Bōsai to Kushiro Unsen" *Shoga kottō zasshi*, No. 358 (April, 1938).

34 See Murayama Yoshihiro, "Kameda Bōsai no 'Unsen sanjin bōmei' ni tsuite" (Regarding Kameda Bōsai's "Unsen's Epitaph") and Agawa Masamichi, "Kameda Bōsai no 'Unsen sanjin bōmei yakuchū" (Transcription and Notes on Kameda Bōsai's "Unsen's Epitaph"), both in *Chūgoku koten kenkyū* (The Journal of Sinology), No. 26 (Tokyo, 1981).

35 For a further discussion of the *ch'in*, its symbolism and its history in China and Japan, see Robert van Gulik, *The Lore of the Chinese Lute* (Tokyo, 1940).

36 According to one author, Bōsai played a T'ang dynasty instrument at the home of a friend, and even constructed (or more likely had constructed) a *ch'in* for his patron Baisō. See Hasegawa Ryōzō, "Kameda Bōsai no kin" (Kameda Bōsai's Ch'in), *Shoga kottō zasshi*, No. 278 (1931).

37 This is an allusion to the Sumidagawa, which flowed through Edo near Bōsai's home.

THE FINAL YEARS IN EDO 1812-1826

Although a house had been prepared for him in Kanasugi and his friend Hōitsu now lived nearby, Bōsai's return was greatly saddened by the news that his granddaughter had died. He wrote to Yajima that he had been deprived of an old man's joy by her death from smallpox at the age of five. Nevertheless, he complied with various requests for calligraphy and book prefaces. He now received enough writing fees so that he no longer lived in poverty, but he refused to consider himself a professional calligrapher. He would not, for example, write *tehon* (model books for calligraphy students). He simply led his own life without concern.

Walking drunkenly, I don't realize my cap is askew.
The spring wind applauds my traveling song.
Children understand, and shout together,
Laughing and pointing at the drunken scholar
* of Kanasugi.*

Figure 4 Tani Bunchō (1763-1840),
Portrait of Bōsai, 1812, Collection unknown

Bōsai renewed his friendships with the literati of Edo; his portrait was painted by Tani Bunchō in the fourth month of this year, although only a reproduction survives (figure 4). Bōsai's inscription shows his ironic self-appraisal:

This old man's head is Japanese, his eyes are
* Japanese.*
—Who are you? What's your name?—
Look closely; Bōsai is not a servant,
Not a merchant, not an artisan, not a farmer,
Not a samurai, not Taoist, neither Buddhist nor
* Confucian.*
Scholars drink wine all through their lives,
But do not serve the government until death.
Is this foolish? Is it wise? I regard myself as
* absurd!*

Bōsai and Bunchō had a delightfully reciprocal relationship. One day when they met, Bunchō painted a folk deity of longevity and Bōsai painted a gourd to hold wine. Bōsai then inscribed Bunchō's painting:

The old man of the South Pole does not record
* his longevity;*
He has long life but does not know long life,
He achieves old age but does not know old age,
Not knowing long life, not knowing old age,
Truly he is the old man of longevity!

Bunchō in turn inscribed Bōsai's painting:

Old man Bōsai does not record his drunkenness;
When drunk he does not know he is drunk,
When sober he does not know he is sober,
Not knowing whether he is drunk or sober,
Truly he is a drunken old man![1]

One day the wealthy merchant Osawa Nagayuki invited Bōsai and Bunchō to a drinking and haiku party along the Sumida River. Also present were Hokuzan and Hōitsu's lover Shōran, who had been a courtesan in the Yoshiwara district and was noted for her artistic skills. They each wrote haiku that evening. Hokuzan was perhaps least comfortable with the form; his verse sets the scene but does not show any originality.

Meigetsu ni   *Viewing Mount Fuji*
Fuji o miru nari   *in the light of the full moon—*
Sumidagawa   *Sumida River*

Figure 5 Tani Bunchō (1763-1840), *Landscape Screen*, 1812, Private Collection, Japan.

Bunchō added Tsukuba mountain to his haiku:

Fuji Tsukuba   *Fuji, Tsukuba—*
Sumidagawara no   *from Sumida River banks,*
tsukimi kana   *viewing the full moon*

Bōsai, perhaps more comfortable with the haiku form, added a playful touch of humor to his verse.

Sumidagawa   *Fishing with nets on*
ami shite aki no   *the Sumida River, we*
ku o etari   *catch autumn haiku!*

The guest most accomplished at haiku may well have been Shōran, and her poem has several touches of subtlety. The "flower-rain" is usually a springtime drizzle; here she implies that she may be the flower, perhaps alluding to her life as a courtesan.

Hana no ame   *A rain for flowers;*
nurenaba nure yo   *if I get wet, I'll be wet—*
Sumidagawa   *Sumida River.*[2]

This kind of poem-party was an important feature of the cultural world of Edo, and Bōsai could now enjoy such gatherings with his many close friends.

Bunchō was achieving great renown as an artist at this time. There was great demand for his paintings, and many of his landscapes were brushed quickly and roughly, with strong compositions and a dramatic variety of ink-tones. A monochrome screen of 1812 can serve as an example of Bunchō's style in his mature years (figure 5). In comparison, an undated landscape by Bōsai demonstrates the differences between the two artists (No. 22), although this is as close to Bunchō's style as Bōsai ever attempted. Instead of building up forms almost exclusively through line, Bōsai added washes in varied tones of grey ink, perhaps under the influence of his friend. Nevertheless, the total effect is quite different. Where in Bunchō's screen the rough and raw quality of the brushwork is balanced by a complex composition in which a number of mountain peaks cluster together, in Bōsai's scroll the forms are simpler and depend more upon outline. Bunchō utilized a great range of ink-tones, while Bōsai clarified his forms by more use of blank silk within the mountain shapes. There is something fanciful about the leaning cliffs in Bōsai's landscape, and his mood is more serene and perhaps more cerebral. The linear strength of the tree-trunks shows his training as a calligrapher, while Bunchō's dependence upon wash demonstrates his delight in pictorial effect.

Bōsai's landscapes are those of a scholar-painter. His compositions are dramatically simplified, his brush-line is generally even and restrained, and the total mood he evokes is remote and tranquil. Bunchō's paintings, although so various as to defy classification, tend to be more technically skillful, fuller in composition, richer in colors or ink-tones and more immediately compelling. His landscapes are often impressive and sometimes seem overwhelming. Bōsai's paintings, on the other hand, are to be savored in serenity.

In the sixth month of 1812 Bōsai suffered a mysterious sickness; he also heard at this time that his

22 Kameda Bōsai, *Mountain Landscape*

friend Kitajima Hokuzan, born the same year as Bōsai, had died. Bōsai later wrote to Yajima:

From the first part of the fifth month I suffered from cold, and lay in bed for sixty days. At this time my hands trembled so much that I could not manage to write a letter, but finally on the tenth day of the seventh month I managed to get out of bed. I cannot say that I am healthy, since my old body is weak and I cannot walk outside my house. After Hokuzan died, I also expected to die, but fortunately I seem to have survived.

Bōsai wrote a gravestone inscription for Hokuzan, expressing his great admiration for his friend's accomplishments. He also contributed one preface to a book of poetry by Hōitsu, and another for a book on flower arranging and scent by Teishōsai Tazuma. The following year of 1813 Bōsai wrote prefaces for books on haiku poetry, travel journals, literary works and historical records. He also inscribed paintings and composed memorial texts. Closest to his heart may have been his introduction to a collection of Sung dynasty poetry edited by his friend Tachi Ryū-an. It is clear that on his return to Edo Bōsai was not forgotten, but became more famous and sought-after than before. From this time onwards, Bōsai was so well-respected as an artist that he had unending requests for examples of his brushwork. Forgeries of Bōsai's painting and calligraphy also appeared, a sign of the artist's success. Bōsai's distinctive style in brushwork made him seemingly easy to copy, although the forgers did not have either his skill or his creative genius. Examining three hanging scrolls of calligraphy, two genuine and one a fake, can help one understand the salient qualities of Bōsai's art.

All three works are undated, but follow the style of Bōsai's mature period. The first, *Old Trees*, is a quatrain written in three columns of cursive script upon an absorbent Chinese paper (No. 23).

23

Old trees are imbued with the face of spring;
Cold waterfalls arouse mysterious reverberations.
I am thinking of a mountain hermit,
Who can appreciate the wind and dew without restraint.

The second genuine work is an eight-line poem written in four long columns of calligraphy (No. 24). The paper is somewhat absorbent, and the style indicates that it may have been written slightly later in Bōsai's life.

24

I don't complain that my books and sword are gathering dust,

I can abandon things of this world as my body grows old.
Planning to go out for a stroll, I cut myself a staff,
In order to live quietly, I search for silk mats.
Cloudy pines and misty bamboo are my guests,
The moon over the mountains and wind on the lake are my hosts.
Do not be surprised by innumerable calamities—
Life right now is the cause of what will come afterwards.[3]

The forgery (No. 25) would seem to fit between the two genuine works in style, since the brushwork is less thick and strong than the former example and less dry and crystalline than the latter scroll. At first it is not difficult to admire the copy, as the line seems very free and bold. Why is it considered a forgery? A few reasons are technical: the paper is of lower quality than usually chosen by Bōsai, the seals are alternate versions of genuine examples, and the seal ink is a slightly different color than it should be. The real problems, however, come from the calligraphy itself. Several characters were written in mistaken forms of cursive script, the columns waver more than Bōsai would have allowed, and the slickness and ultimate flatness of the ink is quite unlike that from the brush of the master.

25

Comparing individual characters can help demonstrate the differences in brushwork. The word "mountain" in the first scroll was begun with a vertical dot; the brush thereupon almost left the paper while moving horizontally, and the character ends with a vertical dot swinging down in a clockwise motion (figure 6). In the second scroll, the word "mountain" again was begun with a dot and a thin-to-thick horizontal line, but this time the brush continued around without leaving the paper; it did pause, however, to produce angular as well as curved movement (figure 7). In the forgery, the character "mountain" is made up of two curved lines, brushed smoothly with no trace of tension or resolution (figure 8). The form lacks both internal strength and external balance.

The same observations can be made for the character "wind." In the first scroll, the strong vertical of the opening stroke is balanced by the curved movement of the brush thereafter (figure 9). In the second scroll, the entire character shows "dry-brush" technique; the slight diagonal of the opening stroke helps to balance the total form (figure 10). In the forgery, the decorative and curving brushwork displays superficial attractiveness at the expense of structural integrity (figure 11).

A further examination of these three scrolls could show many more telling comparisons. The real strength of Bōsai's writing comes not from his fluency, although one may notice this at first, but from his

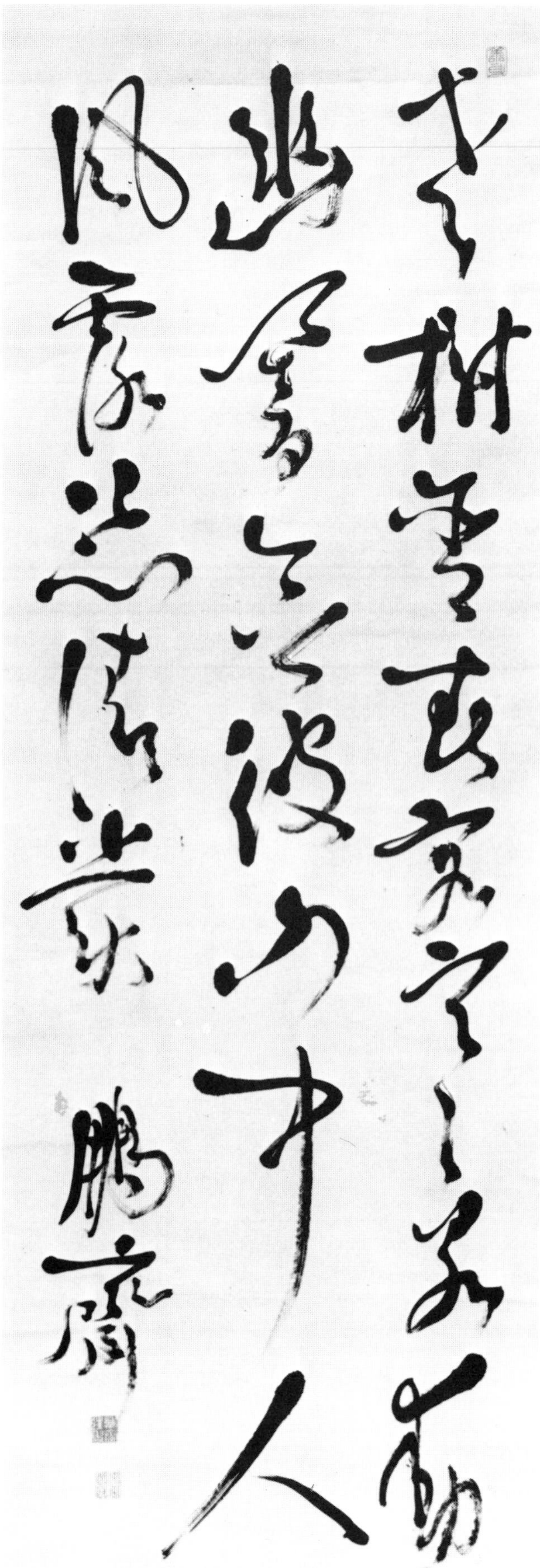

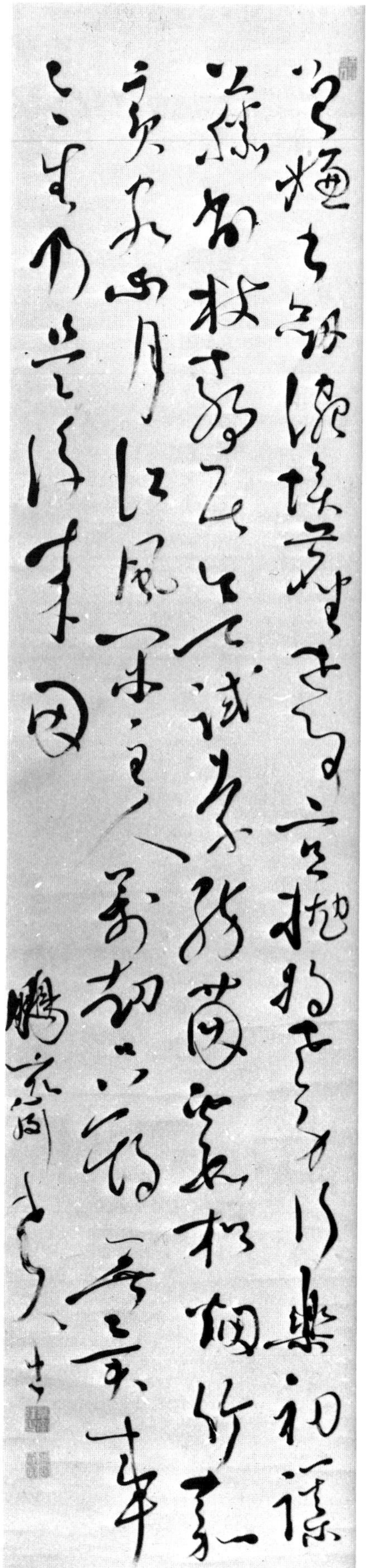

rhythmic pulsations of angles and curves, wet and dry brushwork, tension and release. He shows much more variation in line width than does his copyist, and a more subtle sense of composition. Ultimately, the calligraphy in the forgery is like a flacid ribbon, twisting and turning without purpose, while the genuine writing seems to dance, moving now faster and now slower to an ever-varied rhythm like that of nature itself.

Connoisseurs of fine brushwork in Edo recognized Bōsai's expertise, and he was called upon for inscriptions to be carved on stone. One impressive example, still standing, celebrates one of the beauty spots of Edo, the garden of a rich merchant who planted a magnificent array of plum trees. Bōsai's essay was composed in the second month of 1814,[4] and the text was carved onto a large stone slab and placed in the garden, where it still stands.[5] A translation of the inscription (No. 26), which is full of recondite allusions to earlier literature on plum trees, is given in Appendix A. For this important commission, Bōsai wrote in formal regular script, with the influence of clerical script suggested by the angular shapes and square forms. Bōsai's study of the T'ang dynasty masters Ou-yang Hsun (557-645) and Yen Chen-ch'ing (709-785) can be seen in the architectonically balanced forms and the fleshy full-bodied lineament, but the knife-like strokes and sharply cut angles are reminiscent of earlier inscriptions from the Five Dynasties period. This calligraphy is evidence of Bōsai's great skill in formal style, less recognized than his mastery of cursive script.

The following month, Bōsai brushed a dramatically simple painting with a long inscription in regular script to honor the eightieth birthday of Shiroi Chūka (1735-after 1814). Bōsai chose the pine, a symbol of longevity, as his theme in both poem and painting (No. 27).

The spirit of the wood grows up to the blue sky,
Vigorously curving for months and years into its
    old age.
Its unbending trunk endures in the frost,
Its green beard will not wither in the snow.

23 Kameda Bōsai, *Old Trees*

24 Kameda Bōsai, *Growing Old*

25 Signature of Kameda Bōsai, *Cursive Calligraphy*

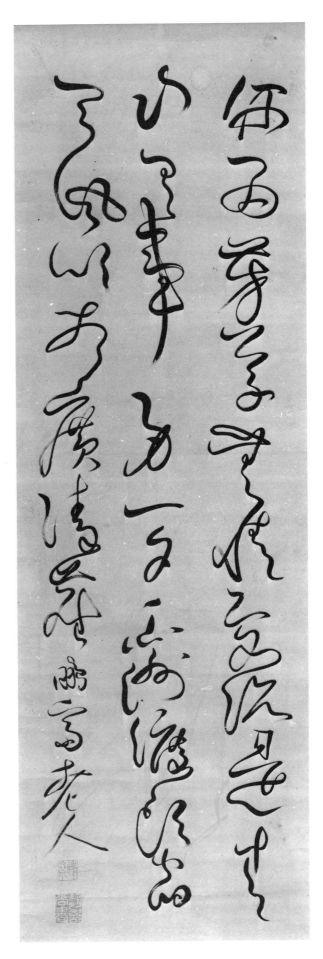

 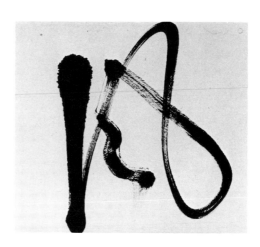

Figure 6 Kameda Bōsai, *Old Trees*, detail "Mountain"

Figure 7 Kameda Bōsai, *Growing Old*, detail "Mountain"

Figure 8 Signature of Kameda Bōsai, *Cursive Calligraphy*, detail "Mountain"

Figure 9 Kameda Bōsai, *Old Trees*, detail "Wind"

Figure 10 Kameda Bōsai, *Growing Old*, detail "Wind"

Figure 11 Signature of Kameda Bōsai, *Cursive Calligraphy*, detail "Wind"

墨花梅莊記

墨花心頑葛陂之傷荒園鋤而新園成植之梅一百株每歲首立春傳信之便步
二月啟蟄之節樹三着花滿園如雪望之則若白浪翻空若蓬來銀闕在水底而
不可近也若藍田美玉簇之駢峙而生煙也蘇東坡所謂花如海益是類耶輒笑而
袤豐張幕塞竇又性大廈植三十株而稱天下之奇焉莊主曰鞠塢幽人風流瀟
好事之士也自初抱梅終十年遂為都丁第一奇觀之場巨鐺大肶酒賞之故
其始衷終焉於是雪之日月之夜雨之朝風之夕今玆觀之春欲觀其開謝皆來寓目
扵此而花之書怒憂覺形態性情之變靡不畢究其快矣陰晴晚照皆衰寓窮
醉而寢忽夢一大姬自稱花孃之膚透如冰骨瑩如玉韻洛一同靚妝一夕月丁酌
從天女降于崑耶城放旐翁愛海棠自稱曰海棠頓今光生酷愛梅花戕命扵
佳人也花孃謂余曰昔陸放翁愛海棠頓其光生同其趣則更甚扵
心生曰梅花頓夫海棠艷矣頓扵清與頑之味如仙禽飲之條覺
心生曰顏我見其清鳥乃使一美人耳鶻而勤主孤燈繡范氏接譜而批之乃謂
光生之枕頭有咳聲俄然夢醒回視無人唯見擢主孤燈繡范氏接譜而批之乃謂曰梅花頓之名獨
輕也枕頭有咳聲俄然夢醒回視無人唯見中前見語心且謂曰梅花頓之名獨
余曰光生無乃見鬼耶何呻吟心長余以夢中前見語而谷時之化十一年甲戌春二月十五
主貴當之非吾凡骨所能任也遂書其言而谷時之化十一年甲戌春二月十五
鵬齋龜田興撰幷書

*In the morning it holds the beautiful mist and
    drips immortal dew,
In the evening it resounds like a jade flute
    in the wind.
People say that this man is as old as the pine,
So I use this image to describe the patriarch.*

*—I have painted this "Straight Trunk and
Curved Branch" for Shiroi Chūka in the third
month of 1814 to congratulate him on his
eightieth birthday—old man Bōsai Kō*

Bōsai was considered a complete literatus at this period of his life. In the free-and-easy artistic atmosphere of Edo, he was called upon by friends and acquaintances of all kinds to assist them in many forms of scholarly endeavor. He wrote prefaces to an ever-growing variety of books, including biographies of famous people and seal-carving compendia. His own *Kyūchū mokyō*, which had been written in 1800, was published on Sado Island. Perhaps what Bōsai most enjoyed was meeting with like-minded friends, such as the poet Kan Chazan who came to visit in the autumn of 1814; they drank wine and recited poems together.[6]

In 1815 Bōsai's friend Hōitsu decided to commemorate the one hundredth anniversary of Ōgata Kōrin's death by assembling and publishing a pair of volumes illustrating one hundred paintings by the great Rimpa master. Although Hōitsu had been born too late to have been a direct pupil, it was from Kōrin's works that the young artist learned the Rimpa painting tradition. Bōsai was called upon to write a preface, in which he stressed the lofty character of both Kōrin and Hōitsu, as well as their excellence as painters.[7] A complete translation is given in Appendix A.

Another interesting task Bōsai undertook in 1815 was writing a preface to a handscroll celebrating a drinking party held for the master of the Nakaya Inn, on the road to Nikko.[8] Ōta Nanpo inscribed at the beginning of the scroll "Bad guests and drunken arguers are not allowed."[9] Tani Bunchō and his adopted son Tani Bun'ichi (1787-1818) contributed paintings to the scroll and the poet Ōkubo Shibutsu (1766-1837) added a verse. Bōsai wrote that the cups of *sake* were so huge that it took two hands to lift them, and described how one hundred drinkers took turns in testing how much they could imbibe.[10] Bōsai himself did not join the contest; although he loved wine, apparently he could not drink very much at any one time.

1816 was a banner year for Bōsai. His book *Kyōchūzan* (Mountains in My Heart), was published,

27 Kameda Bōsai, *Straight Trunk and Curved Branch*, 1814

28a Kameda Bōsai, *Waiting for Fish in the Green Verdure*

and has remained one of the most celebrated of all Japanese woodblock volumes of landscape designs.[11] According to Bōsai's epilogue, on the fifteenth day of the third month a group of scholars gathered together, each taking the brush to write out a poem or a painting.[12] After everyone had taken a turn, a drinking bout ensued. When Bōsai was somewhat intoxicated, he ground more ink and produced a series of landscape paintings. The publisher Izumi Yashōjirō happened to be present, and he took the paintings home with him and printed the book from these designs.

It may be that the actual circumstances were more complex. The pages of the book bear a number of different Bōsai seals; he was unlikely to have taken them all to the party, so it may be that he collaborated with the publisher over a period of time to produce the finest designs possible. In any case, the simplicity and lofty spirit of Bōsai's landscapes ideally suited the woodblock medium, and the cutting of the blocks and printing of the subtle colors were masterfully handled.

The first preface was written by Kikuyu, the master of the Plum Villa. He noted that Bōsai had transformed the boundaries of the Drinker's Paradise into paintings, and the paintings were further transformed by contemplation in Bōsai's heart. Bōsai then added another preface modestly stating that the scenes depicted were merely the mountains within his heart, personal and original, following no method. They stemmed from his "shameful drunkenness," and were brushed only for his own enjoyment and entertainment.

One of the most striking designs in the album is *Waiting for Fish in the Green Verdure* (No. 28a). A sage sits with his pole under two trees and a pavilion; the left side of the composition is almost bare, but begins a diagonal of empty space that points directly at the fisherman. The block-cutter was able to reproduce Bōsai's dry crumbly outlines with consummate skill, and the printer has mastered the effect of soft color washes, but the most notable feature of this landscape is its crystalline serenity. The fisherman waits timelessly; the pavilion will always be empty and the two trees will never lose their foliage. Bōsai has written the title in regular script, balancing with

28a

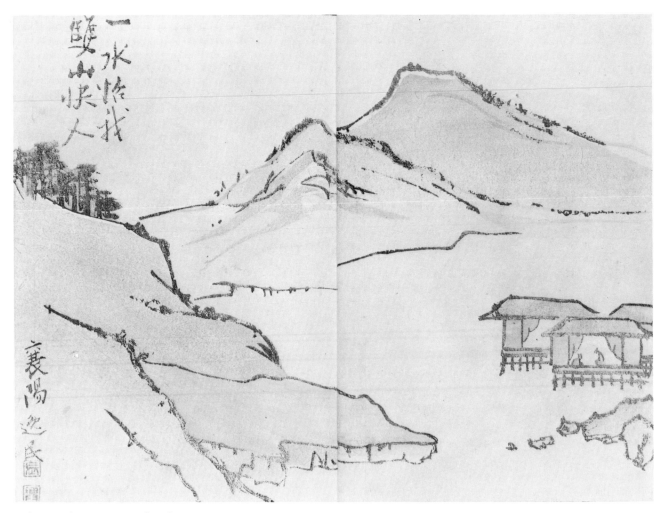

一水怜找雙山快人

襄陽逸民

28b Kameda Bōsai, *A Single Lake*

his signature ("Old man Bōsai") in cursive script in the lower right.

28b Another strong design with an effective use of asymmetry and empty space (No. 28b) is graced by a couplet in the upper left:

A single lake harmonizes the mind;
Paired mountains give pleasure to mankind.

Two friends sit in a hut built on pilings over the lake, enjoying a quiet conversation, but the dominant element is nature. The hills, mountains, rocks and a plateau, rendered with a minimum of interior lines, are distinguished by soft shades of rose, blue and yellow colors. Trees appear only in the upper left, under the poem; their soft greenery helps to balance the blue rocks in the lower right.

28c In *Rivers and Mountains Awaken the Heart* (No. 28c), there is no human presence; a mountain and land-spit extend diagonally from the left, with a cluster of reeds, signature and seal placed in the lower right for balance. Grey mountains in the distance add a sense of depth, but the predominant feeling is of tranquility and emptiness. Yet nothing is perfectly still—the mountain leans, the rocks emerge from the water, the reeds bend in the breeze. It is this ability to combine timeless forms floating freely in space with a sense of life and movement that gives Bōsai's landscape designs their unique and haunting expressivity.

Many of the scenes in the *Kyōchūzan* are printed on single pages, so that two are visible when the book is opened. In one such pair of designs, the right side shows a scholar and his servant under a pine tree (No. 28d). The title *Playing the Ch'in Brings* 28d *Inner Harmony* informs us that under the servant's arm is the musical instrument beloved by scholars and poets. The simplicity of the composition is en-livened by the adroit combination of diagonals, such as the pine trunk leaning to the left and the three clusters of needles arranged in a diagonal to the right. The artist has signed this design "Dadako" (lazy and indolent), the name he had given a friend in 1807 but still occasionally used himself.[13]

On the left, Bōsai has entitled his composition *Rivers and Mountains Rescue My Poetry* (No. 28e). 28e The strong asymmetrical design is arranged in diagonals, and the artist has signed himself "The old

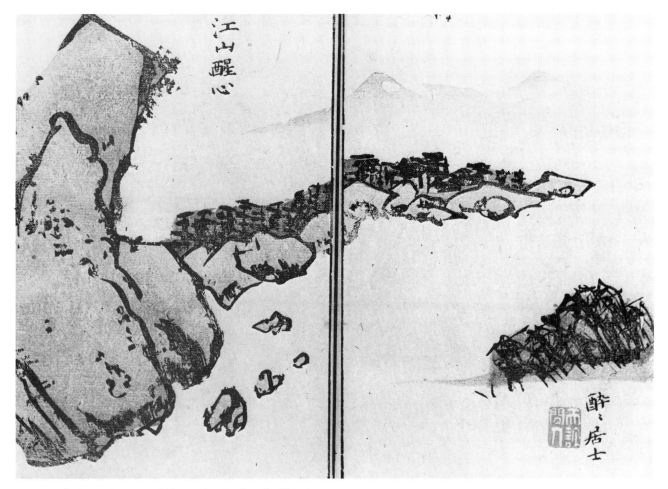

28c Kameda Bōsai, *Rivers and Mountains Awaken the Heart*

fisherman of the ink river." Bōsai also painted a large hanging scroll with the same design, *Alone Viewing the Cold River* (No. 29). Because of the added vertical space, the cliff on the upper left now extends upward and we see its peak, but in other respects the composition is remarkably similar. Instead of enlarging all the details to fit the tall narrow format, Bōsai has kept the size of the seated sage very small, emphasizing the grandeur of nature.

Another example of a woodblock design and painting with similar compositions can be seen in the *Bridge Between Two Cliffs* (No. 30) and a print (No. 28f) with the couplet:

Green mountains charged with jade,
Azure waters suffused with pearls.

The print repeats only the lower central part of the painting's design, adding a more diagonal thrust to the parallel faces of the cliffs. While the painting is one of the most strongly brushed and inked of Bōsai's landscapes, the print is more soft and delicate in mood, but no less striking in design. Although it cannot compete with the painting in terms of wet blurred ink-tones, it achieves an evocative mood of its own with flavorful additions of blue, yellow and green tones to the rose wash of the cliffs.

Opposite the print is an ethereal design, *Yearning for a Pleasurable Place* (No. 28g). Here we see two scholars conversing on a high plateau, with distant mountains barely visible through the mist. Nothing could be more simple, but the composition is enlivened by strong and rhythmic brushwork, soft colors, and an asymmetrical design. In this kind of work Bōsai does not wish us to admire his artistic skill; instead he brings forth the joy of the sages in their lofty conversation.

The *Kyōchūzan* was so successful that a number of editions were printed, utilizing different paper stocks but maintaining a high quality of production.[14] The book, however, provided aspiring forgers with an invaluable opportunity to produce "Bōsai" paintings with strong and pleasing designs. Since Bōsai himself did not brush as many works as a professional artist, the percentage of fakes among his extant landscapes is relatively high. One example is based upon the

28d Kameda Bōsai, *Playing the Ch'in Brings Inner Harmony*

28e Kameda Bōsai, *Rivers and Mountains Rescue My Poetry*

28h
31

woodblock design, *Fishing Alone in the Cold River* (No. 28h). The forgery (No. 31) borrows this composition, but adds a poem in calligraphy that attempts to copy Bōsai's regular script. The comparison of painting and print offers a valuable opportunity for connoisseurship. In the print, the outlines of the cliff are strongly rendered in a dry crumbly line, with only a few parallel interior strokes to suggest volume. In the painting, there are too many similar lines without rhythmic variety. The print establishes a relationship between the fisherman and the tree through countering diagonals and adroit placement. In the painting, the tree lacks firm definition and does not visually relate to the fisherman, who seems unnecessarily small and is not well-placed in the total composition. Furthermore, the forger was too rough in his depiction of reeds, and his use of wash is obtrusive rather than subtle. Most basic of all, the brushwork does not have the personal expression of Bōsai; lines alternate between thin and thick in too regular a rhythm, and the shapes that they define are too similar to each other. The print, despite its much smaller size, has a good deal more visual impact.

Certain technical features also help prove the painting to be a copy, including the lack of strength in the calligraphy and the variant seal-impressions. Although Bōsai's individualistic and seemingly simple landscape style attracted a number of forgers, no one could match his unique brushwork.

The words "mountains in my heart" were used again by Bōsai in one of his most delightfully odd and interesting ink paintings (No. 32). A design that seems almost to parody the classic compositions of the Yuan dynasty master Ni Tsan was rendered in wet, almost blobby brushwork. Underneath the lonely pavilion and sparse trees, tall cliffs were simply depicted in outline, yet the forms seem to bend and move with animistic energy. Bōsai's quatrain in cursive script is his clearest definition of his landscape art.[15]

My painting from its inception has had no method,
How can it be appreciated in this world?
Merely showing a calm and relaxed feeling,
It depicts the mountains in my heart.

The artist signed this work "Uninhibitedly painted by Bōsai." We might suspect that this landscape was brushed after imbibing more wine than usual; in its simplicity and appreciation of nature's creative power lies the essence of Bōsai's art.

Despite Bōsai's enjoyment of evening *sake* parties, he also loved to watch the sun rise over the Sumida River. The view was especially fine from a Shintō Shrine not far from his home, as celebrated in a 33 quatrain written on silk in cursive script (No. 33).

Before the Shirashige Shrine: misty waves at daybreak—
The morning swells run deep and broad in the fresh rays of dawn.
Due east, I suddenly see at the horizon
The red orb of the sun shining unrestrained over the entire sky.

The calligraphy shows Bōsai's prowess in his individualistic "earthworm" script, twisting and turning effortlessly and yet invigorated by the balance of rhythmic tension and release.

Although Bōsai's style in painting and calligraphy was quite unlike the more elaborate and varied art of his contemporaries, he was well-appreciated in Edo. In a compendium of famous personages published in 1816, Bōsai was listed as the "ōzeki" (champion) of eastern Edo, followed by Shibutsu and Bun'ichi. The champion of the western section was Tani Bunchō, followed by the poets Kikuchi Gozan (1772-1855) and Ichikawa Beian (1779-1858). It is ironic that Bōsai, turning his back on competition and refusing to strive for worldly success, achieved what he had forsworn. He remained modest, however, as a poem of 1817 makes clear:

For sixty-six years I have availed myself of the wine-pot,
Ashamed that my talents do not allow me to call myself a scholar.
My secret aspiration is to enjoy my leisure, not to be an old sage;
I live with my loneliness, recovered from sickness.
I don't need to practice Zen meditation to extinguish delusion,
Or to grind medicines in order to be in good spirits.
My house is poor, I use every penny for wine—
I call myself "The Drunken Scholar of Kanasugi."

29 Kameda Bōsai, *Alone Viewing the Cold River*

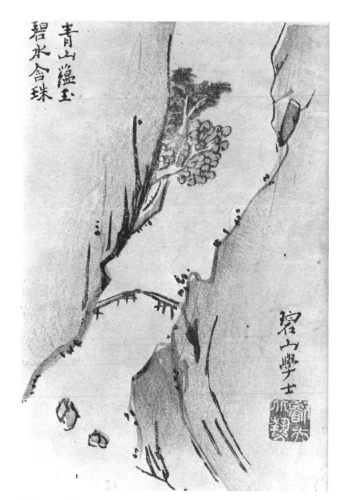

28f Kameda Bōsai, *Green Mountains and Azure Waters*

During these years, Bōsai was able to enjoy nature despite living in the city, as his home retained its rural flavor. His poems celebrate the seasons with an affecting simplicity. One summer day, his entertainment was a pair of butterflies.

Butterflies Flutter

Butterflies flutter
Butterflies flutter
In the south garden, in the north garden,
Through the slender grasses—

They follow each other,
Face each other,
Turn back and forth—

One pair flies past the hedge,
Then returns again—

Butterflies flutter
In the bright spring day.

30 Kameda Bōsai, *Bridge Between Two Cliffs*

In contrast, his poems describing autumn and winter suggest Bōsai's solitude.

Autumn Evening

Autumn: a lonely old man living in a samurai
*   house—*
From time to time falling leaves enter the
*   wind aslant;*
Living in poverty with a reed mat and gourd,
*   I have no visitors,*
In my chilly garden, only a camelia is blooming.

Last night, the cold was oppressive—
This morning, snow covers the mountains.
Dawn comes, pulling up the red sun,
From indigo fields, jade gives birth to mist.

Snow

Last night, lonely flakes of snow—
This morning, my three paths are submerged.
Disliking the scars left by wooden clogs,
I shut my gate and don't venture out.

For the spring, Bōsai wrote a poem which he inscribed on a fan in his distinctively free cursive script (No. 34).

The hundred birds all have their time to sing,
But the voice of the cuckoo never ceases.
When the chilly spring evening is silent,
It cries out alone under the midnight moon.

Bōsai arranged his composition on the fan by giving alternate columns four and one character each. This emphasizes the final word of each poetic line, "time," "ceases," "silent" and "moon." The curving shape of the fan serves to act as a counterpoint to the circling lines of the calligraphy; the total effect is free and bold.

Another fan with smaller characters again alternating four and one per column, was written on patterned paper (No. 35). A counterpoint is brought forth between the wave design and the meaning of the poem. It was originally composed by the Chinese scholar Ku Fei-hsiung for a Korean named Park, who was about to return to his homeland after a long sojourn in China; the tone is melancholy, suggesting that the Korean may find himself lonely even in his own country.

You left your homeland in your youth—
Now, ready to return, you are already an old man.
A guest in a lonely boat, you have dreamed
Of the rivers and mountains east of the ocean.
A great tortoise dives, shaking the banks at the
*   shore,*
Dragons battle in the distant sky.

28g Kameda Bōsai *Yearning for a Pleasurable Place*

You have learned the Chinese language:
When you return, who will understand you?

Why did Bōsai write out this Chinese poem rather than one of his own? Perhaps it held a personal meaning for him, since Japanese scholars of Chinese art, literature and philosophy shared Park's dilemma to some degree. Bōsai's own poetry was only readable by the educated elite who had studied Chinese-style verse.[16] Despite his success with admirers of literati arts, he may have felt some lack of communication with most of his countrymen, and so this poem may have touched him in a special way. The calligraphy seems restrained, partially by its small size against the strong patterns of the paper, but it twists and turns on the curving format with refined elegance.

The year 1819 was a busy one for Bōsai. It included a visit from his friend Suzuki Bokushi from Echigo, who wrote the couplet:

I occasionally search out Bōsai Sensei:
The nest of the phoenix is in a cool bamboo
*   grove.*

71

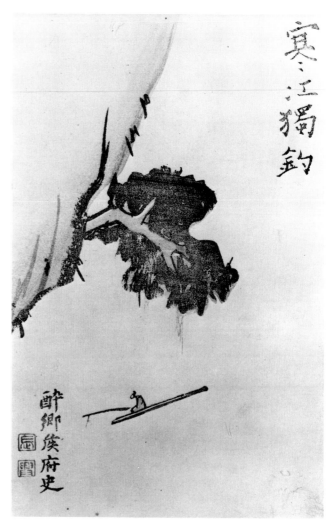

28h Kameda Bōsai, *Fishing Alone in the Cold River*

The peaceful and rustic life in Kanasugi, however, was full of activity. On "horse-racing day" (the eighth day of the second month), Bōsai wrote one of his rare haiku.

Hatsu uma ya—	*On horse-racing day,*
Edo ippai no	*Edo is full of*
harugasumi	*spring mist*

Tani Bun'ichi, the adopted son of Bunchō, had died the previous year, so Bōsai was called upon to write an epitaph. His proudest commission, however, was to write out a long text to be engraved on stone (No. 36) commemorating the "Forty-seven *Rōnin*," (masterless samurai) who avenged their master's unjust death. This story captivated the attention of the Japanese throughout the Edo period, in part through

36

31 Signature of Kameda Bōsai, *Landscape*

32 Kameda Bōsai,
*Mountains in My
Heart*

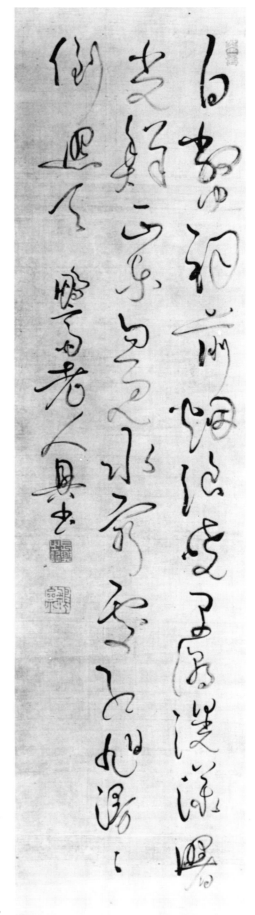

33 Kameda Bōsai,
Shirashige Shrine

34 Kameda Bōsai, *The Voice of the Cuckoo*

theatrical representations, and it remains one of the great human dramas in Japanese history.

In brief, the *daimyō* of Akō, while rehearsing a ceremony in the Shogun's palace, was insulted by Lord Kira, a high official who had not received a sufficiently generous gift for his instructions in etiquette. The *daimyō* drew his sword and wounded his instructor. Baring a weapon in the palace was a grave offence; the *daimyō* was ordered to commit ritual suicide and his estate was confiscated. Forty-seven of his followers waited for two years until suspicions of revenge were abated, then they attacked the castle of Lord Kira and took his life. Having accomplished their purpose, they surrendered to the Shogunate; a great debate then ensued. On one hand, the *rōnin* had followed the Confucian edicts of loyalty. On the other hand, the murder of a high-level official could not be ignored. Although the Shogun himself favored clemency, the *rōnin* were ordered to commit suicide; their bodies were allowed to be buried at the temple of Sengakuji. The moral issue continued to be debated in following decades, and Bōsai was

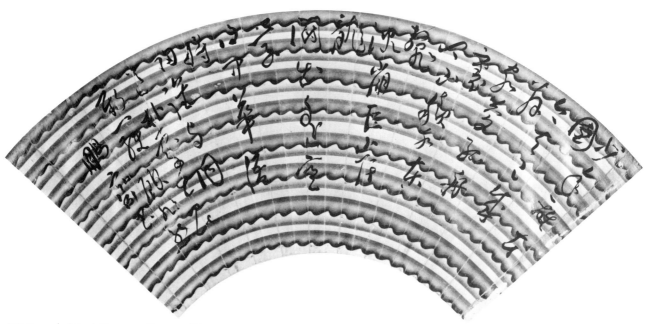

35 Kameda Bōsai, *Poem on Patterned Paper*

36 Kameda Bōsai,
Forty-seven Righteous Samurai, 1819

37 Illustration to the *Myōmyōkidan*, 1821

highly honored at the request for an essay to be carved on stone. In a letter, he called it "the enterprise of a lifetime", and noted how difficult and expensive the project became for its organizers.

Bōsai felt deep emotion at the *rōnin's* self-sacrifice; since their hearts were pure and they willingly submitted to their fate once the revenge was complete, he violently disagreed with people who considered them rebels. In his text, which is given in Appendix A, Bōsai lauds the *rōnin* and their Leader Yoshio as exemplars of moral as well as physical courage.[17] For his calligraphic inscription, Bōsai chose to write in regular script with a hint of influence from clerical script, recalling Chinese memorials of the Six Dynasties and T'ang periods. It is clear that Bōsai took both the composition and the writing out of the text with utmost seriousness.[18] This monument remains the artist's most impressive example of calligraphy in a purely formal style. The characters are well composed, and the quality of the line, even in the rubbing, is crisp and strong.

Bōsai's inscription about the *rōnin* quickly became celebrated in Edo.[19] It occasioned the ultimate accolade, parody; in 1821 a satiric book by a poet named Ōkawara Kibun (1773-1831), writing under the pen name of Sukoppei, was published with the title *Myōmyōkidan* (Strange and Curious Discussions). Various literati of the day were parodied, such as Shibutsu and Beian, but first and foremost in the book was Bōsai.[20] The author imagined that the leader of the *rōnin*, Yoshio (also known as Ōishi Kuranosuke) came back from the dead to visit Bōsai. Included in the volume was a depiction of the two men, showing Bōsai scratching his head in puzzlement (No. 37).

Yoshio Teaches Bōsai

Bōsai rises in the afternoon. The previous day's drunkenness has gone, so he takes up the bottle and is drinking by himself when someone knocks on the door. "Who is it?" he asks. "Someone from nearby Shiba" is the reply, "Can you please give me just a few moments of your time? I've come here to talk with you if I may" the visitor stated quietly. Seeing him, Bōsai wondered who on earth he could be, with a crest on his robe of double-commas with hemp plants above and below. The guest had a sense of dignity and strength without personal concern. He

37

seemed familiar, but Bōsai could not recall having met him. "What is your name?" he asked. "You don't know me, which is natural, for I am Ōishi Kuranosuke from the Genroku period. Now you have kindly written a stone inscription at Sengakuji, and I've come to talk with you." Bōsai praised his visitor, saying "Your loyalty has spread throughout the entire country, and shines like the sun and moon, day and night; one cannot admire you too much. Your story is carved in stone so that later generations can know my humble feelings."

To these modest words, Ōishi replied "Our behavior was natural for loyal retainers, but regarding the peace of the nation, if lords or followers neglect the way of a samurai's heart it would be very strange. I do not worry about fame in these later times; to insist upon loyalty no matter what the circumstances leads to this kind of thinking. By the overflowing sympathy of the abbot, our severed heads were taken to Sengakuji and buried, so that for all of us, our souls could have a resting place. Our long-lived and cherished desire for death was welcome, nothing could compare with it. However, without our intention, this event was taken up in the <u>Bunraku</u> theater and we soon became famous in Edo, Kyoto and Osaka; even in villages scattered here and there our loyalty is praised. Children of two or three years have heard of our loyal actions. Every year on my death anniversary people come to visit my grave in the temple grounds. This is not what I would like, and these days all this attention is excessive.... We already have a gravestone without your inscription, of which everyone is aware. I wonder if anyone is unhappy that it lacks your calligraphy? Now that your own inscription exists, who is happy? The important thing is that our forty-seven graves are lined up together, owing to the previous abbot's great sympathy. That this act was not censured by the government is due to the grace of the Buddha. In erecting another stone marker, what are the officials thinking of? Rubbings of the front side can be sold for money to buy and drink a good deal of <u>sake,</u> I suppose. When the drunkenness fades, you can hold calligraphy and painting parties in Edo, where Tani Bunchō can raffle away fake paintings in order to make enough money to drink until dawn.... Please think about these things."

Despite the biting satire of this book, the stone attracted so much attention that government officials grew nervous and had the carving obliterated, but in 1910 the text was again carved at the order of the Bureau for the Preservation of National Characteristics, and the new stone was erected near the older effaced memorial at Sengakuji.

Towards the end of 1819 Bōsai was asked to write a preface to a twelve-volume set of books on calligraphy, the *Gyōsho ruisan* (An Encylopedic Compilation of Running Script). This was the project of Seki Kokumei (1768-1835) and his son Seki Shiryō (1796-1830), and was so complex an undertaking that it was not actually published until 1833, after the deaths of Bōsai and Shiryō. The volumes contain myriad examples of characters, arranged by the number of strokes, following Chinese calligraphers of different ages. Bōsai's preface is important because it gives his views on the different scripts as well as on the proper models to study; he took a classical stance, admiring the styles of Wang Hsi-chih (307-365) and Yen Chen-ch'ing. Bōsai also noted that this set of volumes, the first devoted completely to running script, presented a "generous and rich sampling" of the extremely varied stylistic possibilities; for a complete translation, see Appendix A.

The *Gyōsho ruisan* was one of many publications on calligraphy printed during the latter half of the Edo period, demonstrating widespread interest in the subject. Among the large number of Japanese calligraphers of the early nineteenth century, Bōsai was one of the most admired, and requests for his brushwork were many. One of his more ambitious works from this period is a six-fold screen with T'ang dynasty poems written in cursive script (No. 38). Bōsai chose texts of which he was fond; the first poem (on the right) expresses his own attitude towards officialdom.

*To my eyes, carriages and official hats
    are no more than feathers of a goose—
If people speak ill of me to the Emperor,
    I have no care.
Taking off my official robe,
    I return to the east;
Blue clouds [high aspirations] are not as lofty
    as white clouds [the free hermit life].*

The calligraphy shows the full maturity of the artist. Although brushed with great freedom, the columns are well-spaced, each character maintaining its internal balance, and the total rhythm is relaxed and easily flowing. There is no trace of vulgar ostentation; variations in line width avoid "static thickness" and the refined brushwork shows no trace of "gross coarseness." Character shapes seem to be reinvented spontaneously, showing natural tension and release without striving for effect. The various tilts to the characters help give the screen an overall sense of movement, but each panel and each word can be enjoyed separately. This form of cursive script, based upon that of Huai-su of the T'ang dynasty and

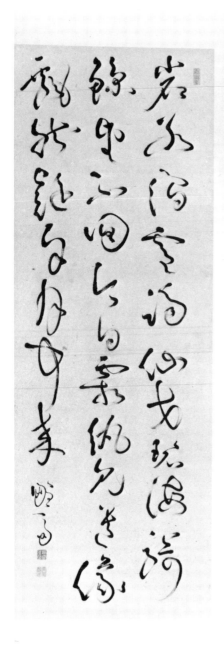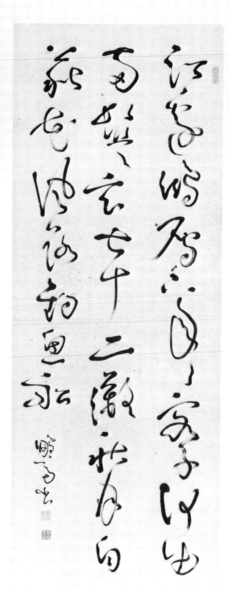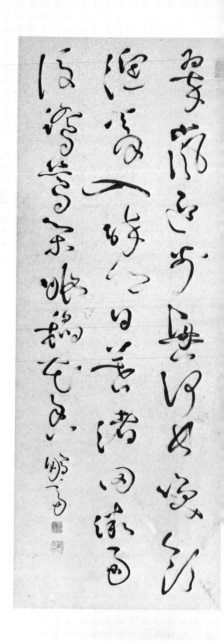

38 Kameda Bōsai, *T'ang Dynasty Poems*

possibly influenced by the monk Ryōkan, had now evolved into a highly personal style which caused Bōsai to be recognized as one of Japan's great masters of calligraphy.

The Japanese *kana* syllabary was originally developed from cursive script, eventually forming its own aesthetic. In his final years, Bōsai occasionally wrote in Japanese, mixing Chinese characters with *kana*. One such example, dated to the fourth month of 1820, is a depiction of a *Gourd*, utilized to carry wine for picnics and other outdoor entertainments 39 (No. 39). The diversity of their natural shapes led literati to admire such gourds, some of which were inscribed or made the subjects of poetry. Bōsai has painted the gourd, possibly his own, with nonchalant skill, and added a poem about Sarashina, the noted Japanese beauty spot, and the Chinese wine-loving poets Li Po and Liu Ling.

> *Without <u>sake</u>, Sarashina with its moonlight,*
> *snow and flowers is just another place;*
> *Without <u>sake</u> to drink, Li Po and Liu Ling*
> *were just ordinary men.*

Bōsai inscribed the painting as brushed while drunk, but the excellence of the brushwork of both painting and poem belies his words. Perhaps he was

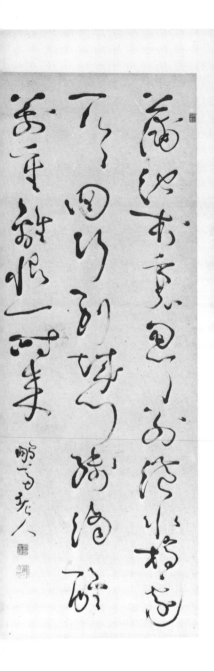
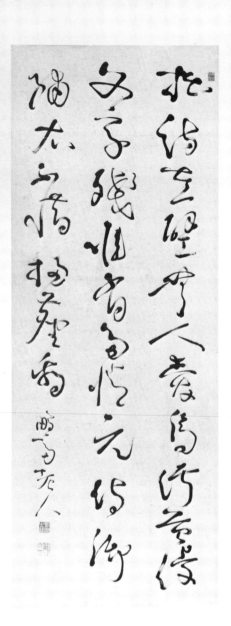
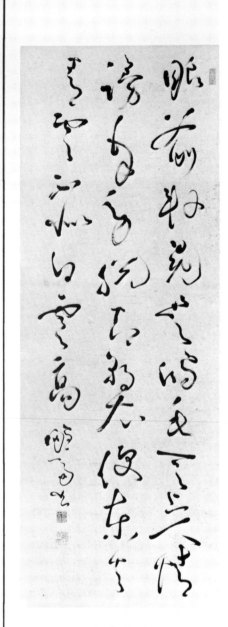

mildly intoxicated, enough to feel inspired but not so much as to impair his brush control. The one trace of tipsiness might be in the character for "man" or "men" which ends the penultimate column, just to the left of the top of the gourd. This character, originally a pictograph of a body with two legs, seems to wobble slightly in a most bibulous manner.[21]

Wine was certainly important to Bōsai, as his poetry makes clear:

> *Sake is good for banishing melancholy,*
> *And useful for forgetting grief;*
> *In our lives we need think only of wine—*
> *What else need we praise?*

Other poems, however, show that wine represented to Bōsai a Taoist element in his thought, recalling Chuang Tzu's story of the old tree that was too twisted and bent to make straight planks for a carpenter, and was thus able to live on when more "useful" trees were being cut down. In wine, Bōsai found an aid to renouncing ambition and accepting the world as it is.

Smiling at Myself

> *This clumsy old man has leisure*
> *   while talented men grow weary,*
> *In this difficult life,*
> *   it is good to long endure.*

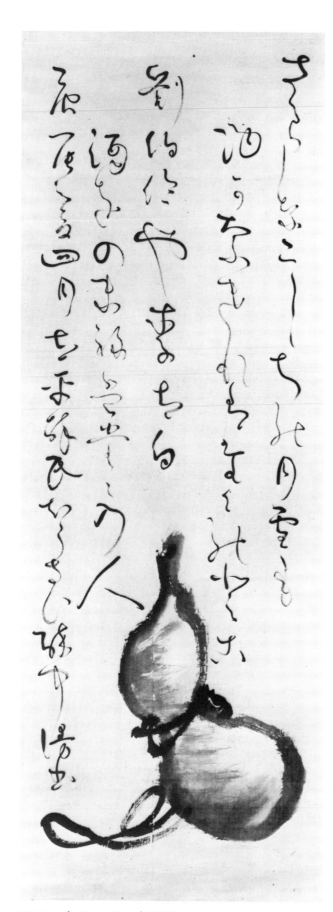

39 Kameda Bōsai, *Gourd*, 1820

*In my lofty drunkenness,
    all is as nothing to me,
I smile at myself—
    who was I in my former life?*

Another poem develops this idea more fully, referring at the end once more to Liu Ling, one of the "Seven Sages of the Bamboo Grove" who had a boy follow him around with a shovel to bury him on the spot when he died. This was an example of great eccentricity, since proper burial was important in China, but Bōsai went even one step further:

Drunken Words

*Mankind is always anxious over worldly
    oppositions,
This old man continuously rejoices in the
    companionship of wine.
When sober, drink, when drunk, sing; why
    should I worry?
Serving the country or being rejected, I forget all
    such cares.
With complete drunkenness, months and weeks
    pass by unnoticed,
I stagger around not knowing even my own body.
The world of wine is like the primordial chaos,
The life of drinking is crazy and free as the wind.
Originally the guest of green mountains and
    white clouds,
If I die of drink, why should I care if I'm buried
    or not?*

One of Bōsai's most interesting combinations of painting, poetry and calligraphy is a representation of an *Abalone* (No. 40). Here the Taoist imagery continues, as Bōsai has playfully reinterpreted a story of Chuang Tzu. In the old legend, the Emperors of the north and south seas wished to repay the Emperor of the central regions, Chaos, for his kind hospitality. Noting that he had no orifices for seeing, smelling, hearing or eating, they thought they would help him by boring one hole in his body each day; on the seventh day he died. Bōsai changed the Emperors' domain to East and West, and added two more holes to conform to the abalone's configuration.

40

*Who divided the primordial chaos,
    and threw this creature into the bottom of the
    sea?
It has only half a body,
    but still exists within the natural law.
After the reward from the Emperors
    of the east and west,
It has nine holes
    where traces of the chisel can still be seen.*

By correlating Chuang Tzu's story with the painting of the abalone, Bōsai has shown a sly wit, poking fun at those who try to improve upon nature. He further suggests that the primordial chaos may have been more vital and creative than mankind's organization and stratification of the elements in the universe.

Another allusion to Chuang Tzu appears in Bōsai's 41 two-word calligraphy, *To Know Fish* (No. 41). The story, which contrasts clever argument with intuitive knowledge, has been translated by Burton Watson.[22]

> *Chuang Tzu and Hui Tzu were strolling along the dam of the Hao River when Chuang Tzu said, "See how the minnows come out and dart around where they please! That's what fish really enjoy!"*
>
> *Hui Tzu said, "You're not a fish—how do you know what fish enjoy?"*
>
> *Chuang Tzu said, "You're not I, so how do you know I don't know what fish enjoy?"*
>
> *Hui Tzu said, "I'm not you, so I certainly don't know what you know. On the other hand, you're certainly not a fish—so that still proves you don't know what fish enjoy!"*
>
> *Chuang Tzu said, "Let's go back to your original question, please. You asked me how I know what fish enjoy—so you already knew I knew it when you asked the question. I know it by standing here beside the Hao."*

The calligraphy is one of Bōsai's simplest and most evocative. The word for "know" has been simplified to two strokes, one merely a dot, and the total effect suggests the kind of intuitive "knowing" that art rather than logic can convey.

In 1821, Bōsai reached the age of seventy by Japanese count, and his pupils held a party for him in the first month. Bōsai's New Year's poem reiterates his love for wine and his distrust of ambition.

Drinking Song for the New Spring

In this world it's better to be drunk than sober,
After all, what purpose is there to live without
   wine?
From the past to the future is all a dream,
What point is there to cleverness or foolishness?
The virtuous Po I and the villain Tao Chih
   share the same grave,
All over the world, tombs pile up over each other.
After my death, my fame will last as long as
   spring flowers—
A lifetime of profit and loss? Just a game.
One hundred years is not a long time,
Longevity or early death, riches or poverty are
   matters of fate.
Suffering cannot be prevented, what use is it
   to weep?

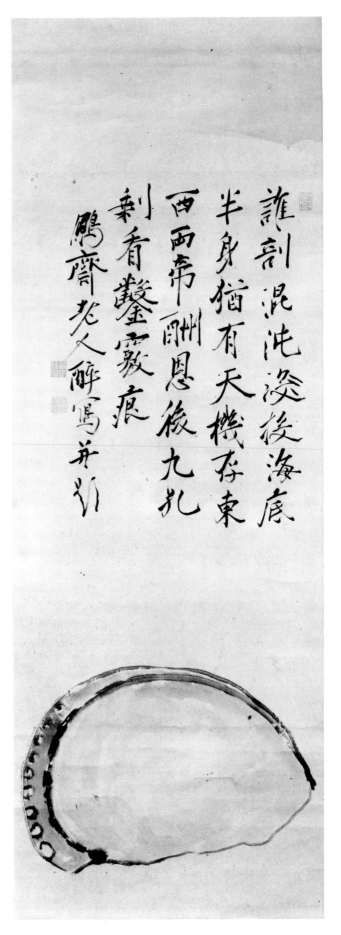

40 Kameda Bōsai, *Abalone*

41 Kameda Bōsai, *To Know Fish*

Figure 12
Anonymous,
Portrait of Bōsai,
1821, Private
Collection, Japan

Within ourselves we are not entirely virtuous.
As I regard the vast universe,
There is no reason not to get completely drunk.
Pawning my winter clothes for enough money,
I buy a bottle of wine so I may welcome the
    spring.
As I drink, my singing is boundless,
As I drink, my mouth opens with laughter.
For me, this pleasure is enough,
There is no need to proclaim my literary
    accomplishments.
Let's ask to hear the first song of the New Year—
We don't have to worry about recording these
    drunken words.[23]

At the banquet in his honor, Bōsai was highly
praised by his friends, prompting him to compose
another poem with the preface:

In 1821 during the first month of spring upon
my retirement, my children and pupils prepared
a celebration to congratulate me.

This worthless scholar is ashamed at the praise
    of his advanced age,
But I rejoice in tranquility at this longevity
    feast.
Still trying to explain the classics, I am old
    but not yet dead;
Lucky to be healthy, I am still good at
    drinking.....

Who said this old scholar is poor?
I can still celebrate and drink with my old friends.

A portrait was painted of Bōsai at this time (figure 12), over which he inscribed a poem saying that during the course of his seventy years he had never sought after fame or profit, but merely enjoyed wine and avoided worry. He did not cast blame upon others and had no shame over his activities; when he died he would have no complaints.

One of the pleasures of old age is meeting with friends, and in Edo Bōsai was able to enjoy many such gatherings, which frequently resulted in co-operative works of art. One of the most elaborate of these is a *gassaku* (joint art-work) involving ten different poets and painters (No. 42). It was entitled *Gathered Clouds* by the calligrapher Nakai Tōdō (1758-1821), a former pupil of Hokuzan. In order of probable execution, Tani Bunchō began by depicting a plum tree in the lower right and Sakai Hōitsu added a moon in the upper left. The dove sitting on the plum branch was added by Kuwagata Keisai (1764-1824), an artist of the *ukiyo-e* (floating world) tradition who also studied Kanō school brushwork and eventually retired as a lay monk; he was noted for his wit and individuality. The bending pine tree was painted by another *ukiyo-e* artist noted for his cultural sophistication, Kubo Shunman (1757-1820). Tani Bun'ichi, whose death date of 1818 forms a *terminus ad quem* for the painting, added a few freely brushed bamboo leaves in the lower left, and then the poets took their turns. Bōsai wrote a quatrain referring to the Chinese poet famous for his love of plum blossoms, Lin Pu (967-1028).

Surrounded by rustic huts, the plum trees
blossom one by one,
Half a pond of spring waters reflects their
overlapping shadows.
A crane dances alone within the fragrance—
I realize this must be the home of Lin Pu.

Directly below Bōsai's poem is a couplet by Kikuchi Gozan.

Plum blossoms like snow; full spring in the
town—
We can hear the first chirping voices in the
east wind.

To the left, Ichikawa Beian added a couplet praising spring foliage at dawn:

42

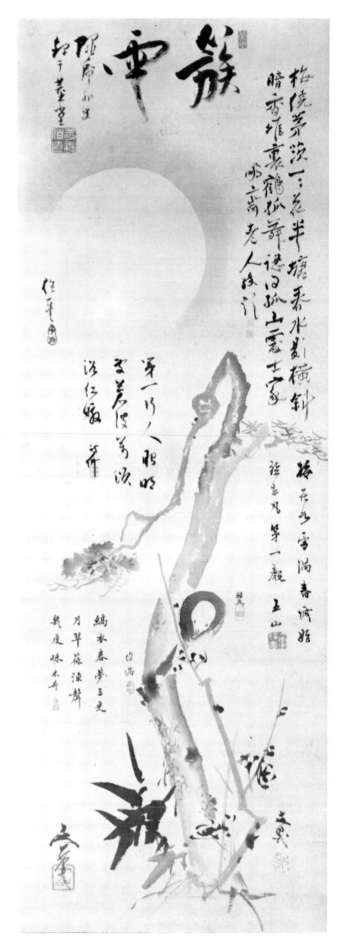

42 Kameda Bōsai and Nine Artists, *Gathered Clouds*

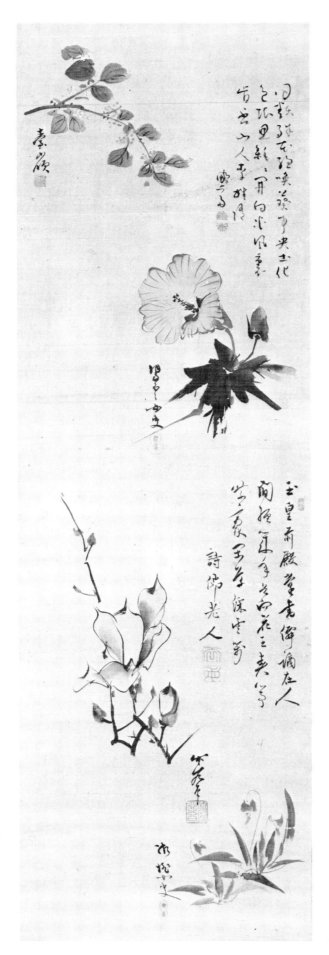

*The first traveler's eyes are brightened
By myriad miles of green waves bathed in the
   red morning sun.*

This combined work may lack unity as an artistic product, but it stands as an example of a cooperative effort by friends of different schools and various talents working together. The cultural world of Edo was indeed diverse; what it may have lost in clarity of definition was more than made up for by the creative vitality and cross-fertilization of such gatherings.

Another such *gassaku* demonstrates that women were not excluded from such events. Perhaps initiated at a party, a combination of four painters and two poets produced a charming scroll of flowers and poems (No. 43). In the lower left, Yamamoto 43 Shōtō (dates unknown), the second wife of Bōsai's friend Hokuzan, delicately painted *sumire* (violets), while above and to the left a more dramatic *mokuren* (magnolia) was depicted by Bunchō's pupil Ida Chikkoku (1790-1843). Next in ascending order, a yellow *aoi* (hollyhock) was portrayed by Yamamoto Suiun (Hokuzan's granddaughter, dates unknown), while near the top, Magata Dairei (a pupil of Nakabayashi Chikutō, dates unknown), added a small spray of white and yellow *hagi* (bush clover).

The poems, which are rather obscure, have been translated by Jonathan Chaves:

*Same species, different flowers, both called k'uei;
The central element, earth, produced their
   memorable color.
Richly flourishing, they open in the midst of
   summer's hot wind;
Are they willing that the mountain recluse
   named Li should follow?*

                        —*Bōsai*

*The immortal in charge of documents in the
   Jade Emperor's outer court
Has been banished to the world of men—how
   many years have passed?
Wishing to memorialize the Flower King on
   matters close to his heart,
With purple brush he leisurely inscribes this
   paper of tinted clouds.*

           —*Old man Shibutsu*

Another combined work on the theme of flowers, dating perhaps to 1818 or 1819, is most unusual (No. 44). It seems that a group of literati in Edo came 44 across a large Chinese print of birds and flowers, actually made of woven paper. This technique is

43 Kameda Bōsai and Five Artists, *Flowers and Poems*

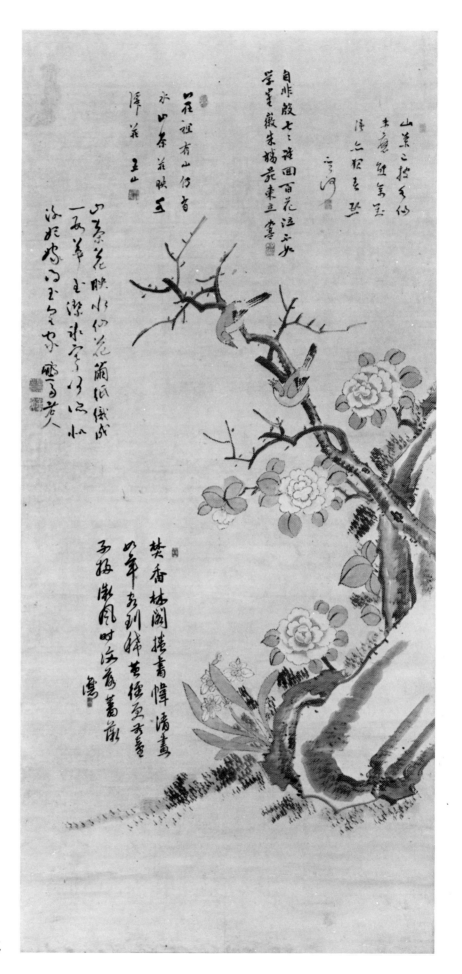

44 Kameda Bōsai and Four Artists,
Poems on Chinese Woven Paper

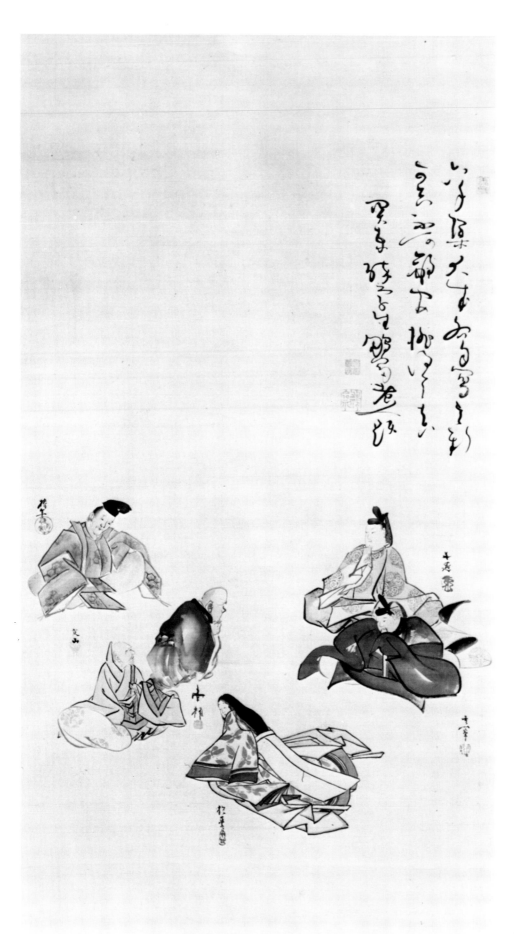

45 Kameda Bōsai and Six Artists,
Six Poets

very rare, consisting of long thin strips of paper woven together as though they were silken threads. The design printed upon the paper strips reveals two birds on a tree branch, with camelias and narcissus flowers below them. Five calligraphers were inspired to add poems in a semi-circle around the design, perhaps beginning with Bōsai on the left. His poem in cursive script makes a play on the names of the camelia ("mountain tea flower") and the narcissus ("water immortal") as though a mountain were reflected in a lake.

The camelias are reflected by the narcissus,
Strips of paper have been woven into several
*   kinds of flowers.*
Pure jade, chill ice, what do they resemble?
The Goddess of the Lo River married to the
*   Jade Emperor!*

Kikuchi Gozan, enjoying Bōsai's play upon words, added a couplet at the top left of the scroll, above and to the right of Bōsai's poem.

Within the flowers there are "mountains" and
*   "waters"—*
The camelias are reflected by the narcissus.

To the right of the Gozan poem, Kashiwagi Jōtei (1763-1819), considered one of the "Four Great Poets of Edo" along with Ichikawa Kansai, Gozan and Shibutsu, added a quatrain. He referred to the T'ang dynasty Taoist Yan Ch'i-ch'i who had the ability to cause flowers to bloom out of season, and to Ts'ui Hui, a T'ang dynasty beauty who sent a portrait of herself to her absent lover and then languished away.

I am not Yen Ch'i-ch'i,
Who was able to reverse all the flower's grief;
So I follow the example of Ts'ui Hui:
A red banner still stands in the eastern garden.

In the upper right of the scroll, Kan Chazan wrote a poem avoiding abstruse literary references.

The camelia is already open,
The narcissus has not yet withered;
Two birds chatter back and forth,
Enjoying the spring warmth.

The comparison between the verses by Jōtei and Chazan demonstrates the two main facets of Chinese-style poetry of the time; one is erudite and depends upon allusions to Chinese legend, the other is a simple response to nature as depicted in the print.

The final poem, brushed in strong running script at the lower left, was written by Bōsai's former pupil Hōjō Katei (1780-1823); perhaps he believed the camelias to be roses.

To the fragrance of burning leaves in my
*   forest hut,*
I roll up a curtain over my books;
The pure day seems to last
*   as long as a year.*
The path is covered with blossoms,
*   but there is no longer a servant to sweep*
*   them up,*
The gentle breeze, time and again,
*   blows down rose petals.*

One of the most venerable of artistic traditions in Japan is that of the poet-portrait. It stems from the even older practice of collecting works by great *waka* masters and including them in anthologies. During the Heian period, painted handscrolls of poets with inscriptions of their most notable verses became popular, and the tradition continued unabated through the Kamakura and Muromachi eras. In the Momoyama and Edo periods, artists continued to portray the great Japanese *waka* masters of the past, but a new spirit of humor was introduced in these paintings by Kōrin and his followers of the Rimpa school. In addition, informal portrayals of haiku poets became a feature of Nanga and Maruyama-Shijō artists, particularly under the influence of Yosa Buson (1716-1784). As well as single portraits and sets of thirty-six masters, groups of two, three or six poets were occasionally combined; one of the most interesting examples bears an inscription by Bōsai (No. 45).

What is most fascinating about this work is that it combines the abilities of Nanga, Rimpa and Maruyama-Shijō school masters. In the more traditional cultural center of Kyoto, this kind of combination would have been most unlikely, and even in Edo it was not common. Bōsai may have acted as a catalyst among the different literati and non-literati artists and poets of the day, encouraging them to come together without the narrow sectarian viewpoints that have often prevented such cooperation. This was in tune with his Eclectic school philosophy, which did not admit the exclusive truth or value of any one system of thought. Thus, the painting of six poets testifies to the atmosphere of artistic freedom in the new capital during the early nineteenth century, and to Bōsai's central position in the cultural circles of the day.

The poet just under Bōsai's inscription at the right, in courtier's hat and gown, was painted by Tani Bunchō in a style that harkens back to Heian and Kamakura precedents. The outlines of the robes are more angular and sharply defined, however, than is usual in the classical tradition. The sole poetess in this group, in the lower center, was portrayed by Sakai Hōitsu. She half hides her face with her sleeve, and although she is clearly based upon an early model of a Heian beauty, the design of butterflies on her kimono is an unusual touch. The two diagonals made by

her body, hair and robe help to unify the painting's total composition, leading visually to the depictions of the other poets.

Above the poetess to the right is a portrait painted by Hōitsu's pupil Suzuki Kiitsu (1796-1858). Although already a master of the Rimpa school, Kiitsu here shows his early interest in Maruyama-Shijō techniques, including the use of broad washes applied with a flat brush *(hake)*. Just above the poetess on the left is a poet brushed in full Maruyama-Shijō technique by Suzuki Nanrei (1775-1844). This style had originated in Kyoto with Maruyama Ōkyo (1733-1795) and was brought to Edo by Ōkyo's pupil Watanabe Nangaku (1767-1833). Nanrei studied under Nangaku, taking the first character of his art name from that of his master, and then helped to popularize the new style in Edo. As exemplified by his poet here, Nanrei often dispensed almost entirely with outline, suggesting the bulk of the form by the use of shaded wash applied with a flat brush. Furthermore, he was the only painter in the group not to choose a classical *waka* poet, instead portraying the haiku master Bashō. Nanrei's depiction of Bashō's homespun robe and pleasantly distorted features is different in both spirit and technique from the portrayals of the earlier court poets.

Above and to the left of Bashō is a court poet painted by another Maruyama-Shijō master, Ōnishi Chinnen (1792-1851). First a student of Bunchō, Chinnen later became a pupil of Nangaku; with Bunchō's tolerant blessing, he converted to the new naturalistic style. Below the figure by Chinnen is a portrait of a monk-poet by Matsumoto Kōzan (1784-1866), a pupil of Bunchō who was also influenced by Hōitsu. Thus, the six painters represent three different schools: Bunchō and Kōzan belong at least nominally to Nanga, Hōitsu and Kiitsu to Rimpa, and Nanrei and Chinnen to Maruyama-Shijō.

Instead of producing a confusing mixture of styles, the six artists brushed a harmonious painting; the pleasing U-shaped composition is relieved from excessive symmetry by the cursive script inscription in the upper right. Bōsai made clear his approval of the diversity and ultimate unity of the six artists when he wrote:

Assembled together by six hands,
Each poet has been individually depicted;
Close to each other rather than separated—
The arrangement is wonderfully natural.

—Inscribed by the drunken scholar of the Kantō, old man Bōsai

46 Suzuki Nanrei and Kameda Bōsai, *Portrait of Bashō*

Another portrait of Bashō by Nanrei, this time on paper rather than silk and including the old poet's traveling bag, is also graced with a Bōsai inscription (No. 46). Once again the haiku master is seated with his head resting upon his hands; here he seems to be dreaming. Bōsai's haiku poem above the figure is especially interesting, since it provides a gentle parody of Bashō's most famous verse:[24]

Furu ike ya   *An old pond—*
kawazu tobikomu   *a frog jumps in:*
mizu no oto   *the sound of water*

Bōsai changed a few words to give the poem a new meaning:

Furu ike ya   *An old pond—*
sono go tobikomu   *after jumping in,*
kawazu nashi   *no frog*

From the expression on the old poet's face, he could well be enjoying Bōsai's new haiku.

A more scholarly painting bearing Bōsai's inscription was painted by two Nanga masters of Edo (No. 47). The bamboo, most popular of the "four gentlemen" subjects, was brushed in free and relaxed style by Ōnishi Keisai (dates unknown). The father of Chinnen, Keisai also studied with Bunchō, but remained faithful to literati tenets of brushwork. The accompanying rock, of a strange and dramatic shape admired by Chinese connoisseurs, was added by Haruki Nanko (1759-1839), a friend of Bunchō who achieved a high reputation as a Nanga master. Nanko made the long journey to Nagasaki to seek out both Chinese and Western artistic knowledge; here his overlapping dry brushwork is clearly in the Chinese manner.

Bōsai's inscription, written "while very drunk," is a poetic couplet praising the bamboo:

The top of the green bamboo joins together
   with the clouds,
Delicate buds and young shoots aspire to reach
   the sky.

While Nanga masters favored Chinese literati themes, Rimpa artists more often derived their subject matter from Japanese birds, flowers and plants. Early in his career, Hōitsu's pupil Kiitsu brushed several such subjects in delicate tones of washes, clearly influenced by Maruyama-Shijō techniques.[25] Bōsai, doubtless to encourage the young painter who lived only a few doors away from his home in Kanasugi, inscribed a

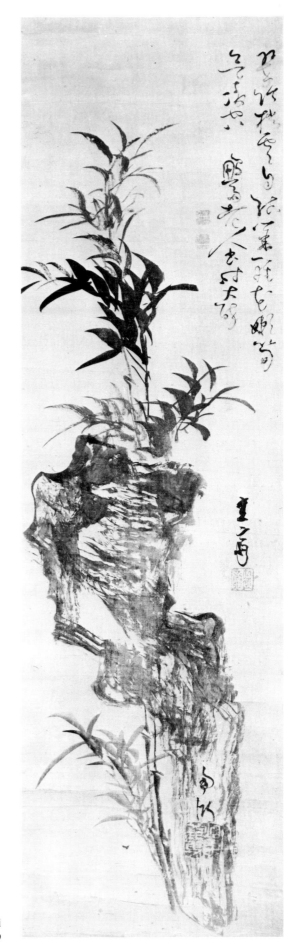

47 Haruki Nanko, Ōnishi Keisai, and Kameda Bōsai
Rock and Bamboo

few of these softly rendered paintings with appropriate quatrains. Here he has referred to the Japanese tradition of weaving a special cloth from arrowroot *(kuzu)* leaves (No. 48).

48

> *Arrowroot leaves hang down from green vines,*
> *Wafting slowly in the warm breeze of the fifth*
> *   month.*
> *While the women work diligently to weave*
> *   <u>kuzu</u> cloth,*
> *They do not know the fragrance will encourage*
> *   us to drink more wine!*

Although the poem is in Chinese characters, it has several Japanese characteristics. First, it refers to *kuzu*, which is one of the "seven autumn grasses." Secondly, it has a strong seasonal imagery, utilizing a local custom in order to bring forth temporal associations. Finally, Bōsai's use of cursive script suggests some of the aesthetics of Japanese *kana* writing, with soft curving strokes and a feeling of modest gracefulness. Kiitsu's delicate tonal shadings within the pleasing composition of the painting, in which the negative spaces of white paper between the forms are as fully developed as the brushstrokes themselves, add to the total effect of an almost tangible summer atmosphere.

Many of Kiitsu's paintings brushed while Hōitsu was still alive combine a modest format and approach with elements of the Maruyama-Shijō style. After his teacher's death in 1828, Kiitsu was to paint more colorful and decorative works, but around the year 1820 it was Hōitsu who enlivened the Rimpa tradition with a new blend of striking design and refined, sometimes meticulous brushwork. *Two Warblers on a Persimmon Branch* (No. 49) shows the boldness of approach that Hōitsu developed in his mature works. The basic compositional design based upon diagonals is not unlike the Kiitsu *Arrowroot*, but the bright red-yellow-orange colors on the fruit and the use of *tarashikomi* (water or color dropped on still-moist areas and allowed to merge) produce great visual drama. Perhaps in response to Bōsai's kindness in inscribing Kiitsu's work, here Hōitsu allowed Bōsai's son Ryōrai to add a poem. Unfortunately the young man omitted one character in the final line, but the quatrain's meaning is still apparent.

49

> *The evening wind blows rain past my forest*
> *   dwelling,*
> *As persimmon leaves turn red, I write*
> *   calligraphy upon them;*[26]

48 Suzuki Kiitsu and Kameda Bōsai, *Arrowroot*

I am full of thoughts of the Hsiao and Hsiang
  Rivers and the ocean—
But for now I am content with a perch to eat
  and a bottle of wine.
                              —Ryōrai Shi the fisherman

The style of Ryōrai's regular script is amazingly
close to that of his father. The characters are angular,
and the line moves rapidly from wet to dry within
a single stroke. There is a bite and flavor to these
brushstrokes that is like the sweet-sour taste of per-
simmons. The only feature that suggests the calligraphy
is from a youthful hand is its rather formal placement in the upper right, sedulously far from any
brushstrokes of the painting. Bōsai might have spread
his characters out in a more relaxed fashion.

Bōsai's own painting at this time continued his
linear tradition, with free-floating forms organized in
diagonal shapes as in his *Cliff Landscape* of 1821
50 (No. 50). The cliffs are now even less structurally
plausible than before, but they provide a visual en-
closure for the lower trees and solitary fisherman.
The painting exhibits a disembodied loftiness that
seems almost hallucinatory. It is as though nature
exists on two levels, a lower human world and another
above it, to which man can only aspire in his dreams.

Another dramatic landscape from Bōsai's later
years is unusual for its bright colors painted upon
the medium of satin, which adds a lustrous white-
51 ness to the painting (No. 51). The most dynamic shape
is that of the foreground tree, which reaches up to
the tall mountains above it. Two sages, one standing
and one seated, converse in a hut built on pilings
over a lake; Bōsai was not afraid to repeat his favorite
motifs, but due to his lively brushwork they are never
exactly the same. Just touching the tallest mountain
on the right, the cursive calligraphy is an important
factor in the total visual effect, while the poem suggests Bōsai's unending pleasure in nature.

Whether mountain colors are near or far,
I walk all day long to view them—
Finding tall peaks everywhere,
This guest of the road does not know their names.

            —Painted and inscribed by old man Bōsai

The strength in Bōsai's brushwork is especially
remarkable in his late years since he was affected by
a form of palsy. He wrote in a letter "for three years
I have been having trouble speaking, and writing is
difficult, but I am glad to say I can drink wine."

49 Sakai Hōitsu and Kameda Ryōrai, *Two Warblers on a*
Persimmon Branch

50 Kameda Bōsai, *Cliff Landscape*, 1821

It may be that from this time, Ryōrai was assisting him in some of his literary compositions, but Bōsai continued to enjoy his wide-ranging interests. In 1822, for example, he wrote a preface to a book on plum blossom painting, quoting the Chinese saying that "calligraphy and painting originate in the same single brushstroke" and praising the exalted resonance of the subject.

Bōsai also was happy in 1822 to write a preface for a book on food and cooking entitled the *Ryōri tsū* (Food Connoisseurship). This volume contains recipes for the various seasons, poems about food and illustrations of fish, vegetables and fruit by such artists as Bunchō, Nanko, Chinnen, Hōitsu and the *ukiyo-e* masters Kuwagata Keisai and Katsushika Hokusai (1760-1849). In one of the prefaces, the owner of the restaurant that sponsored the book explained that he had traveled to Nagasaki to study Chinese foods, and also learned other recipes from friends; one of Keisai's illustrations shows four of these friends at table (No. 52). Facing us with his hand in the air is Bōsai, and to our left is the chubby figure of Shibutsu. Below Bōsai is Hōitsu, with his head shaved as a monk; at the right, holding a wine cup is Ōta Nanpo. This illustration presumably dates from 1822. Bōsai's preface, as translated by Jonathan Chaves, is both scholarly and charming.

The harmonious blending of fine flavors and fragrant smells through the proper use of cooking techniques is a means to bring health to the inner vitality and smooth flow to the breath and blood. The official regulations of the Chou dynasty included methods of cuisine, and the <u>Book of Ritual</u>, *one of the Confucian classics, refers to...ancient techniques of cutting and cooking. This is how attentive [the ancients] were to this matter.*

The great chef Yaozen is the one who first mastered that which we all love. His skill is exquisite, his methods fine, and his fame is great through the capital. Even the kitchens of wealthy landowning families recognize Yaozen. Hence he has brought together a book of recipes for the four seasons in accordance with what is appropriate for spring and autumn, cold or warm weather, as well as cooking techniques and ingredients from sea and land, seasonal and fresh....

An ancient has said, "When a man who loves meat faces a butcher's shop, he'll start chewing." Won't those who read this book happily start chewing away?
　　　　　　　　　—*Written by old man Bōsai*

51 Kameda Bōsai, *Mountain Colors*

52 Kuwagata Keisai, Illustration to *Ryōri tsū*

Late in 1822, a two-volume collection of Bōsai's poetry, the *Bōsai sensei shishō* (A Selection of Bōsai's Poems) was published, edited by his former pupil Nishina Hakkoku (1791-1845).[27] The poems cover a span of many years, but they were not arranged in chronological order and very few are dated. Nevertheless, they present the variety of themes, modesty of approach and personal touch of Bōsai as a poet. A number of examples from this pair of volumes have already been presented; the main themes throughout continue to be Bōsai's appreciation of wine, travel and the beauties of nature. One of the longer poems demonstrates why Bōsai was drawn to paint landscapes with such an individual spirit.

Evening: Sitting in the Mountains

*I have climbed through a thousand layers of clouds
And arrive to sit at the ten-thousand-foot summit.
The wind brings no dust from the capital,
I become one with the sky amidst the greenery.
As the sun sinks, the sky becomes a pure blue—
In the haze, cliffs are a brilliant red.
Myriad rustlings of the wind drown out all other
    sounds,*

*Not a single bird can be seen flitting to and fro.
Evening in the mountains goes beyond loneliness;
With the mind pure, I have no desire to sleep.
The solitary orb of the moon
Shines on the sleeves of my robe.*

Bōsai was considered one of the finest poets of his day, exemplifying along with his friends Hokuzan and Chazan the new trend towards direct personal expression and restrained imagery. With his artist's eye, Bōsai was able to express the moods of nature in various seasons, times of day and different weather conditions. Beyond his ability in pure description, he wrote in such a personal manner that we can sense his complete identification with the world around him; the moonlight reflecting on the sleeves of his robe becomes a symbol of his own inner state of awareness, serenity and unity.

Bōsai reached the age of seventy-two in 1823, the year in which he painted the last of his extant dated landscapes on a folding fan (No. 53). A scholar, old and bent with age, crosses a bridge towards a pavilion on a hill. Half the space on the fan is filled by the cursive script calligraphy of a poem with a melancholy cast.

53 Kameda Bōsai, *In My Leisure*, 1823

In my leisure, I sleep beside the lovers' trees,
Or row out among the intertwined lotus flowers.
Why does the wild goose come to these sand
*   islands?*
For whom does he labor to fly so far?

> —*Poem and painting by old man Bōsai*
> *at age seventy-two*

Whereas many poets have compared the free life in nature with the restricted existence of man, here Bōsai has his own leisure and wonders about the energy and persistence of the wild goose. Autumnal colors in the landscape match the imagery of the poem; the result is a true merging of the "three treasures" of the scholar: painting, poetry and calligraphy.

Although afflicted with palsy, Bōsai could still use his right hand. He was able to comply with many requests for his calligraphy, and could still drink four or five small cups of *sake*. Celebrating his longevity, in 1823 there was a birthday party for Bōsai to which eight or nine hundred people came. One of the guests was the famous *kabuki* actor Danjurō VII (1791-1859), who with his pupils brought thirty containers of *manju* (steamed cakes filled with red beans) as a gift.[28] Bōsai promptly gave Danjurō a sum of money that was much more than the cakes were worth—typical of the old scholar and one reason why he was always poor despite his honoraria for writing.

Later that year Bōsai, Bunchō and Hōitsu went to see Danjurō appearing in one of his most famous roles, that of the swashbuckling hero in *Shibaraku* (Just a Moment), one of the eighteen classic dramas in *aragoto* (rough and dramatic) style. This play, which had been created for Danjurō I in 1697, is notable for the entrance of the hero. Villains are about to take control of a town when the word "Shibaraku" is heard from the rear of the theater, and Danjurō appears on the long walk-way in a dramatic costume bearing his diamond-shaped stacked-box crest.

The performance that the three artists saw was so exciting that they commemorated the event in a *gassaku* (No. 54). The painting, mounted on silk from Danjurō's costume, shows the attributes of the actor. Bunchō painted the long sword with a powerful brushline showing "flying white," while Hōitsu added the fan and the peaked cap of the actor. Bōsai's inscription is written in cursive script:

54

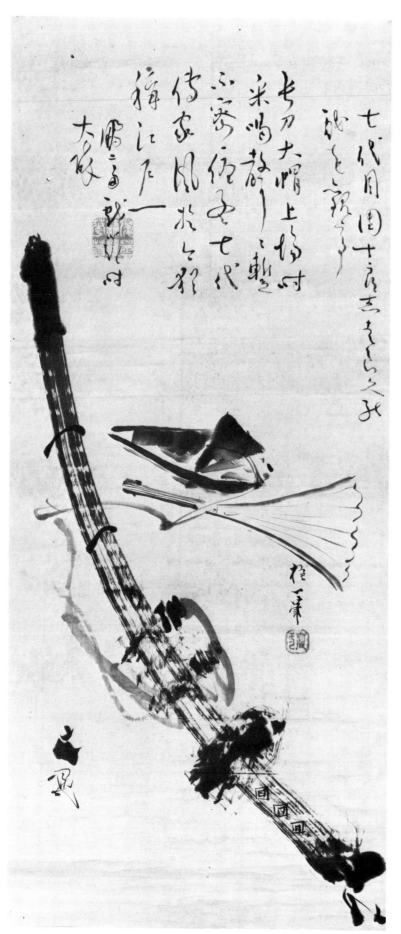

七代目團十良もさくら之み
池を親るゝ

七刀大帽上ゐ時
来鳴なり三軽
ふ窓佰子を七代
傳家風水々名
狩に左一
鳴る戎
大阪

54 Kameda Bōsai, Tani Bunchō and Sakai
Hōitsu, *Shibaraku*, 1823

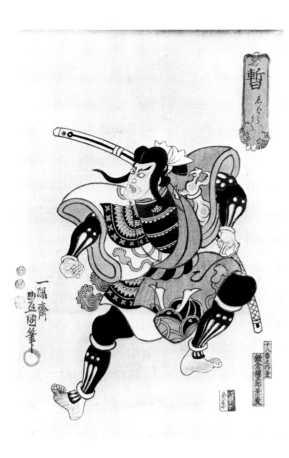

55 Tsunoda Kunisada, *Danjurō in Shibaraku,*
1852

After having contemplated the art of Danjurō VII in Shibaraku: *When the actor has arrived on stage with his long sword and peaked hat, frenetic applause does not stop for an instant [*"shibaraku"*]. In admiration for the tradition of this family in its seventh generation, it is not necessary to say anything more than that today we must consider Danjurō the finest actor in Edo. I have written these lines after getting quite drunk—Bōsai.*

Several woodblock prints of the time show Danjurō VII in this role; the costume and makeup have a visual drama that is extremely effective in the print medium. One of the most interesting portrayals of Danjurō by Tsunoda Kunisada (1786-1864) shows the actor dressed in the original costume for the role, which includes a helmet and a dragon's claw in the design of the robe rather than the more familiar 55 large diamond pattern (No. 55). The actor has just made his entrance with the cry "Shibaraku!" He poses dramatically in the style of his ancestors and crosses

one eye in a *mi-e,* one of those moments of intense stillness that are the emotional highpoints of *Kabuki* theater, causing the frenetic applause noted by Bōsai.[29]

Although probably written earlier, in the summer of 1823 Bōsai's gentle parody of Buddhism, the *Bussetsu maka shubutsu myōraku kyō* (Sutra of the Great Vision of Exquisite Pleasure of the Wine Buddha), was published with one illustration each from Bunchō and Hōitsu. The former shows Liu Ling and his wife worshipping at the altar of wine (figure 13) while the latter is a portrait of Li Po. Having previously suggested in his poetry that *sake* could take him beyond earthly cares, Bōsai here demonstrated his ability to write the same theme in the manner of Buddhist sacred texts. The main difference between this and a real sutra is that Bōsai's deity and his followers are more fond of wine than of ritual. The text is ironic, but by no means anti-religious; Buddhism was still so secure an element of Japanese life that it could withstand, or possibly even embrace, humor about its deities.[30] Bōsai, for example, wrote that the Wine Buddha told the Buddha "This rice juice of mine abolishes all thoughts of self and foolish ideas, and pours over worries....Suddenly everyone is free from the fetters of earthly cares, entering the wondrous pleasures of the drunken paradise....This is the way to complete enlightenment." Bōsai's sutra, which ends with a drunken poem, is translated in Appendix A.

Bōsai became more seriously ill in 1823, but

56 Kameda Bōsai, *Kotobuki*, 1823

his doctor realized that he would not completely recover, and so did not begrudge him wine. Partially paralyzed, Bōsai had difficulty in speaking, but could still hold the brush. One work of calligraphy from this year, written in Japanese, begins with the large character *Kotobuki* (Good Luck) and continues with a five-line poem in *waka* style modestly cele-
56 brating his longevity (No. 56).

Wagatoshi ni	*To say that others*
ayakarekashi to wa	*should reach the same*
	age would be quite
okogamashi	*presumptuous—*
saredomo kotoshi	*nevertheless, this year I*
nanajū ni	*have become seventy-two!*

In the first month of 1824, the year of the monkey, Bōsai painted a monkey on a long pole, with a haiku poem inscribed along the side (No. 57). This is 57 the only painting still extant from the final three years of Bōsai's life. Again it shows his modesty at reaching a ripe old age, hinting that he has stolen the years rather than earned them.

Seijin no	*The cleverness of*
otoshi o kasumu	*the monkey is to grasp*
saru rikō	*the long life of a sage*

After his signature, Bōsai impressed seven of his seals, perhaps realizing that he would be doing few if any more paintings. His brushwork, however, is

98

still firm and graceful.

Despite his poor health, Bōsai continued to be importuned for prose and poetry. A second volume of *Ryōri tsū* was published in 1824; it contains another preface by Bōsai, perhaps partially ghost-written by Ryōrai.

Of those who are outstanding in the field of cuisine in the world, everybody recognizes Yao-zen. He can take a scallion and a slice of meat and create a dish worthy of the immortals' kitchens. He has compiled Ryōri tsū *containing the best recipes for all four seasons and cooking techniques; I wrote a preface for this work. The book has been praised by chefs, and purchasers have filled the shops. People seeking it out have numbered as many as trees in the forest; the woodblocks from which it is printed have come close to splitting. Yaozen has now compiled oral recipes passed down by great chefs as well as some he has thought of himself, and put them together in a second volume. It is even more complete than the first in cooking techniques and ways to mix sauces. He visited me at my Hiei village residence and asked me for another preface. As I flipped through the book, my mouth watered and the saliva flowed—it was as if I had entered the kitchens of Heaven and tasted the forbidden ambrosia there. With this, I poured out some wine from the jar, boiled up some wild vegetables, drank three cups in a row, became quite intoxicated, took up my brush and wrote these words as a preface.*
    —Third day of the second month, spring of 1825, the seventy-four-year-old Bōsai wrote this. [31]

The following year Bōsai's friend Ōta Kinjō died, and Bōsai was asked to write an epitaph. According to one story, Bōsai began the task but did not finish it, commenting that "the human spirit survives forever, we need nothing more. When I die, please do not compose an ostentatious memorial essay." [32]

The year of 1826 began with a great snow and a number of small earthquakes. Bōsai's health declined, and on the ninth day of the third month, he died at his home in Kanasugi. It was the custom for poets to compose a final verse just before their death. One legend remains that Bōsai painted a "Cold Crow on a Dead Tree" and then wrote "Iku tokoro e ikō" (now I will go where I must go) just before he passed away. [33] A more probable story is that he wrote "Kyō wa kore kagiri" (today is limited to this). [34] By Japanese count, he was seventy-five years old at his death. An

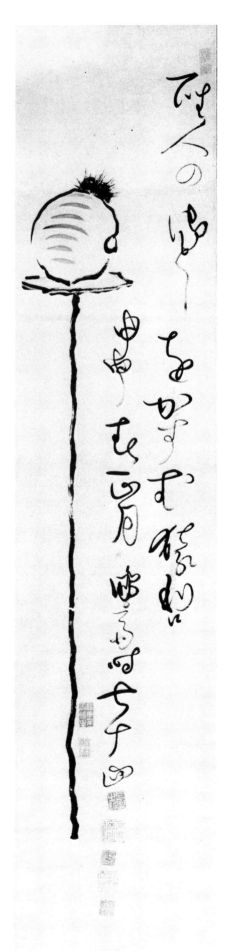

57 Kameda Bōsai, *Monkey*, 1824

58 Suzuki Kiitsu, *Portrait of Bōsai*

59 Kameda Bōsai, *Landscape*

undated portrait of Bōsai by Suzuki Kiitsu may have been painted at this time; it shows the old poet, slightly emaciated in appearance, seated upon a mat reading a book. Behind him are his brushes, inkstone and more scholarly volumes (No. 58). The mounting is covered with impressions of his seals, which were presumably effaced after his death except for two which were given to Nishina Hakkoku.[35] There is an intensity of expression on Bōsai's face that is quite affecting. It suggests the continued vigor of his mind despite the lines on his forehead, cheeks and neck; wine has not dulled his spirit.

In the year of 1827, on the ninth day of the third month, a memorial service was held for Bōsai at the temple of Shōfukuji where he had been buried. Sakai Hōitsu was moved to write a poem:

Bōsai Sensei's First Anniversary Service
in Imado's Shōfukuji

Ika ni sen	*Even after the*
sakashiki hito mo	*most wise and humane of men*
naki ato ni	*has passed away—*
kotoshi mo onaji	*this year, the same as always*
hana zo chirikeri	*the blossoms scatter and fall*

Bōsai was not forgotten in succeeding years. In 1838, Tani Bunchō came across an ink landscape by his old friend, and added a soft rose wash to the undersides of the rocks and blue mountains above the pavilion (No. 59). He then inscribed the work:

Bōsai Sensei painted this; Bunchō added color in the eleventh month of 1838.

Despite its unusual composition and almost ghostly atmosphere, this landscape is fully representative of Bōsai's style. The land, rock and mountain forms were delineated with a minimum of interior "wrinkle" lines, producing an effect of spaciousness and repose. The asymmetrical composition was primarily constructed of diagonals, with the center of interest placed far to one side. Although there is some use of wash, the painting was built up almost entirely with calligraphic line; the strength of the brushwork, ranging from more fully inked strokes to dry crumbly lines, gives the landscape its special flavor. Finally, there is a mood of unworldliness and lofty simplicity in this painting that communicates the personal spirit of the artist.

58

59

1 See Saitō, op. cit., p. 49.

2 Ibid., p. 50.

3 The final line recalls a couplet attributed to Lao Tzu, "Good and bad fortune have no gate, but man himself invites them."

4 The original manuscript has been published in "Kameda Bōsai shinseki shin baisō hiki" (The True Autograph of the New Plum Villa Monument Text by Kameda Bōsai), Sho-en, Vol. 5, No. 2 (April, 1915).

5 The garden remains a beauty spot open to the public, but the plum trees are gone.

6 The following year Tani Bunchō painted the scene of the first meeting of Bōsai and Chazan, which occurred unexpectedly near the bridge at Nihonbashi; Chazan was on his way to a literati banquet that Bōsai had just left in a rather intoxicated condition. See Ihara Kun'ichi, "Chazan Bōsai Nihonbashi kaizōzu ni tsuite" (Regarding a Painting of the Chance Meeting of Chazan and Bōsai at Nihonbashi) parts 1 and 2, Bingo shidan, Vol. 1, No. 5 (1925) and Vol. 2, No. 11 (1926).

7 Today, the Rimpa school is considered overtly decorative, but during the Edo period it was admired by literati as a cultivated tradition, more noble in conception than that of the purely professional schools. In the late eighteenth century, the Nanga painter and theorist Kuwayama Gyokushū (1746-1799) classified two Rimpa masters as part of the Japanese "Southern School" because of their cultural attainments rather than their style as artists.

8 Even Hōitsu, a non-drinker, attended the party, which became so famous that a woodblock was cut and prints sold at the inn celebrating the event.

9 See Udaka Ōha, "Shokusan, Bōsai to Kōyō tōinkan" (Shokusanjin, Bōsai and the Kōyō Drinking Contest Scroll), Fude no tomo, No. 248 (1921).

10 One version of this scroll is now in the New York Public Library. See Sorimachi Shigeo, Catalogue of Illustrated Books and Manuscripts in the Spencer Collection of the New York Public Library (Tokyo, 1978), pp. 56-57.

11 Some copies of this book bear a date of 1809 on the back inside cover, but as the preface and colophon both include the date of 1816, this is regarded as the correct year of execution.

12 The ink used that day had been made by Fei Yu-lu (active circa 1600).

13 It is also possible that this design was brushed before 1807 and later added to Bōsai's book, but it seems more likely that the artist continued to enjoy using this signature upon occasion.

14 See Charles Mitchell, Biobibliography of Nanga, Maruyama, Shijō Illustrated Books (Los Angeles, 1972).

15 A variant of this poem is recorded in Furukawa Osamu, Kameda Bōsai no e ni tsuite" (Regarding Kameda Bōsai's paintings), Shoga kottō zasshi, No. 285 (1932).

16 Although he had been delighted to see his friend Ryōkan write a banner in Japanese syllabary, until the last years of his life Bōsai continued to brush almost all of his poetry and calligraphy in Chinese characters.

17 Bōsai was so imbued with the heroism of the rōnin that he later wrote a preface for a volume in Chinese which published the story of the faithful retainers.

18 The original manuscript is reproduced in "Bōsai no kaisho hi" (Bōsai's Regular Script Memorial Stone), Shodō, Vol. 12, No. 5 (June, 1943). See also Mitamura Genryū, "Akō yonjūshichi gishi to Bōsai sensei" (The Forty-Seven Righteous Samurai of Akō and Bōsai), Nihon oyobi Nihonjin, No. 531 (1910).

19 Bōsai was soon asked to write more inscriptions for stone monuments. See Kayahara Tōgaku, "Sumidagawa ni okeru Kameda Bōsai no nishihi" (Two Stone Monuments Engraved with Poems by Kameda Bōsai Along the Sumida River), Shoga-en, Nos. 1-2, (1924), and a similar article by the same author in Nihon Bijutsu, No. 16 (April, 1930).

20 For more information on Kibun, see Shimpen Saitama kenshi (New Compilation of Saitama Prefecture History) Shiryō hen 12, Kinsei 3, Bunka (Tokyo, 1982), pp. 52-57.

21 This work may have been brushed at a party, as it is not sealed.

22 See Burton Watson, The Complete Works of Chuang Tzu (New York, 1970), pp. 188-189.

23 Nevertheless, Bōsai was asked to write out this poem on a pair of screens in the autumn of that year.

24 Bōsai may have written the same parody on a portrait of Bashō by Hōitsu; see Saitō, op. cit., p. 50.

25 For another example, see Pat Fister's entry on Kiitsu in Stephen Addiss et. al., A Myriad of Autumn Leaves: Japanese Art from the Kurt and Millie Gitter Collection (New Orleans, 1983).

26 This reference is to a Chinese poetess who wrote her verses on persimmon leaves and threw them into the stream; she married the man who found them.

27 See Watanabe Chisui, "Kameda Bōsai to Nishina Hakkoku," Shoga kottō zasshi, No. 277 (1931).

28 Danjurō, as well as an actor, was a man of poetic sensibilities and quick wit. In 1816 he had come to visit Hōitsu on the second day of the second month, a day on which there was a folk custom of exorcising demons by throwing beans and telling the devils to depart ("oni wa soto"). The actor arrived carrying a folding fan, and Hōitsu asked him to write a poem. Danjurō remembered a haiku written by Kikaku about his father:

Ima koko ni	Here comes [the fearsome]
Danjurō ya—	Danjurō—
oni wa soto	devil, go away!

Thus the current Danjurō wrote a witty verse:

Watashi de wa	As for me,
gozarimasen zō—	I'm not at all like that—
oni wa soto	devils go away!

The following day Bōsai came to visit Hōitsu, and saw the fan with the poem. As it was no longer a day to chase away demons, Bōsai added to the fan:

If Danjurō comes after the day of exorcism:

Shichidaime	The seventh generation
nao oni wa soto	is still the devil; go away,
Danjurō	Danjurō!

29 The print is dated 1852, late in the career of Danjurō VII, who had great pride in his family tradition and passed the role in Shibaraku on to his son, Danjurō VIII.

30 For example, in woodblock prints of this time, Buddhist avatars were pictured enjoying the attentions of beautiful geisha and drinking at parties.

31 Translated by Jonathan Chaves.

32 Harada, op. cit., p. 33.

33 Ibid. Another source reports Bōsai's final writing was "Ware masa ni kikyū sento su" (I am now about to go to my rest). See Higashi Kan'ichi, "Kameda Bōsai," Kinsei hyaku ketsuden (Tokyo, 1954) p. 68.

34 Sugimura, op. cit., p. 250.

35 See Appendix B for further information on Bōsai's seals.

BŌSAI'S FOLLOWERS

Bōsai's interest in calligraphy was kept alive by his students. Closest in style to the master was his son, Ryōrai. At first glance it is difficult to distinguish between the writing of father and son; Ryōrai did not have the creative genius of Bōsai in terms of developing a unique style. A single line calligraphy by Ryōrai 60 displays his graceful brushwork (No. 60).

> *Black kites fly,*
> *Fish leap—*
> *How vigorous!*

Many characteristics first developed by Bōsai can be seen here. Most brushstrokes begin with wet blurring dots, but the quick movement of the brush leads to "flying white" at the end of the strokes. There is a tension between angular and curving lines, although perhaps with less boldness of effect than before.

Even closer to Bōsai's style is a horizontal scroll written by Ryōrai twenty-one years after his father's 61 death (No. 61). The calligraphy displays a combination of strength and free movement of the brush, and the poem demonstrates that Ryōrai shared Bōsai's relaxed attitude towards life.[1]

> *When awake, I drink wine, when drunk I sleep—*
> *This method is not heroic, nor is the way to*
> *become an immortal,*
> *But what good would it do to rely on large*
> *amounts of gold?*
> *For a long time, this has been my family*
> *heritage.*
>
> —*Written by Kameda Ryōrai, one day before*
> *the full moon in mid-summer, 1847*

Although he differed from his teacher in style, the most influential of Bōsai's pupils was Maki Ryōkō. Born in Echigo (Niigata Prefecture), Ryōkō came from a small town named Maki, from which he took his family name. He lived near a lake *(kō)* in which there grew many water chestnuts *(ryō)*; the lake itself was shaped something like a chestnut, so he assumed the art name of "Water Chestnut Lake" *(Ryōkō)*. After his parents died when he was young, Ryōkō traveled to Edo to study with Bōsai. The young scholar made great progress in Confucianism, poetry, and especially calligraphy. After the death of his teacher, Ryōkō

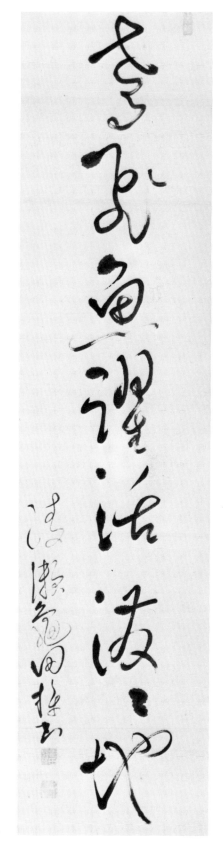

60 Kameda Ryōrai, *Black Kites Fly*

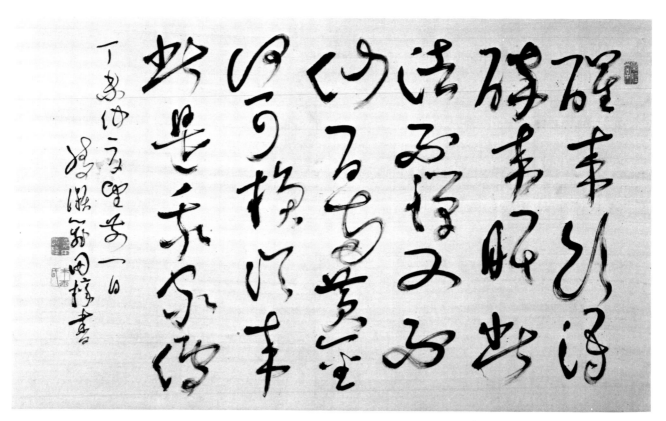

61 Kameda Ryōrai, *My Family Heritage*, 1847

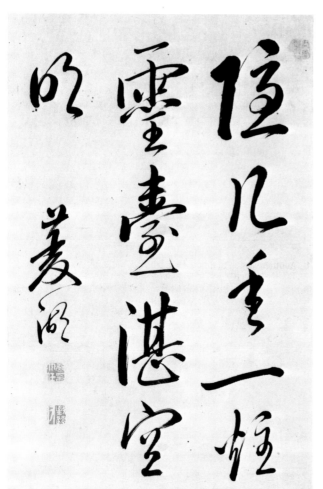

was considered along with Ichikawa Beian as one of the two finest Chinese-style calligraphers in Edo. While Beian had patrons and pupils among the samurai elite, Ryōkō followed the lead of Bōsai in being admired by the townsmen.

Unlike Bōsai, Ryōkō made extensive studies of all scripts, and his calligraphy was published as models for students in a series of woodblock books during the late Edo period. He became a professional calligrapher, and was noted for his thorough studies of early Chinese masters of all scripts. As a result, his calligraphy shows more technical expertise, but less individual personality, than that of Bōsai. A couplet in running-cursive script exhibits Ryōkō's fluid brushwork (No. 62).

62

Leaning on the table with the fragrance of one stick of incense,
My spirit becomes clear, empty and bright.

The writing demonstrates Ryōkō's compositional strength and complete control of line. Occasional strong vertical and horizontal strokes balance the impression of fluent curves. It is apparent that Ryōkō

62 Maki Ryōkō, *Clear, Empty and Bright*

63 Maki Ryōkō, *Tea Song*

has studied not only the early Chinese masters, but also the traditions of Chao Meng-fu (1254-1322) and Tung Ch'i-ch'ang (1555-1636). There is a nice contrast between the tall thin shape of the third character of the first (right) line "fragrance" and the extended horizontal of the following single stroke character "one." Nevertheless, there is a tendency to admire the finesse of the calligraphy more than to absorb the personality of its author.

Another work by Ryōkō displays his expertise in clerical script (No. 63). He ruled out on a piece of silk seventeen columns both vertically and horizontally, within which he wrote the *Tea Song* of the T'ang dynasty poet Lu T'ung (d. 835). This is one of the most famous texts on tea in the Chinese tradition; Ryōkō was undoubtably responding to the Edo period revival of interest in Chinese tea-drinking traditions;[2] see Appendix A for a translation of the poem.

The brushwork is refined without being fastidious. Ryōkō has understood the essential artistic features of clerical script; most lines are even in width and the character forms are generally sharply angular, but for contrast there are curving lines of varying width, particularly flowing down to the right and left. Each word can be seen as a balanced design, but the total effect of the evenly spaced columns shows a sense of antique elegance. This is clearly the work of a master of the brush.

1 Another version of this poem attributed to Bōsai is given in "Kameda Bōsai shinnen shokan" (A Short New Year's Letter by Bōsai), *Sho-en*, Volume 7, No. 3 (January, 1917, unpaginated).

2 Tang dynasty tea was pressed into bricks and then boiled. In the Sung era, tea was often powdered and whisked; this formed the basis of the Japanese tea ceremony. During the Edo period, the Ming dynasty custom of steeping tea leaves in almost-boiling water was known as *sencha*, a tradition which became popular among Sinophiles in Japan.

五
CONCLUSION

One of the joys of art is that it enables us to experience a different world than our own, although the individual spirit of the artist may be surprisingly empathetic. Past ages of faraway countries can be illuminated by studying the deep personal expression of a master, just as a knowledge of an artist's environment can help our understanding of his work. We meet the artist face to face in the experience of his poetry, painting and calligraphy, and through this meeting we may enter his exterior world and share his interior life.

What was the world of Bōsai? His life-span can be divided into four stages: the student, the teacher, the wanderer and the free-spirited literatus of Edo. In each of these stages, his world was different.

As a pupil of Kinga in the Seijūkan, he met the young intellectuals of the city and formed life-long friendships with scholars such as Hokuzan. As a teacher, he was admired for his clarity, brilliance and kindness, but the Shogunate's disapproval of his philosophy led to disillusionment and eventually to the loss of his school. His years of travel opened a whole new world to Bōsai, that of the poet-calligrapher-painter with no official responsibilities. He could savor the beauties of Japanese scenery, and was inspired to compose poetry and paint landscapes in his own unique style. Finally, he found success in Edo as an independent literatus. His circle of friends now included former colleagues and pupils, artists of many different schools, poets, actors, chefs, scholars and calligraphers. He drank *sake* with them, wrote prefaces for their books and epitaphs when they died, and fit in easily with people of all walks of life. He "farmed with his brush," living in a rural area on the outskirts of Edo near his friends Hōitsu and Kiitsu, and survived upon the proceeds of his "writing fees." Although Bōsai never abandoned his scholarship, he came to understand the folly of ambition and the hubris of attempting to change society; he simply enjoyed wine, poetry, art and friendship.

Bōsai expressed his personal feelings in his writings and art. In his verse, whether in Chinese or Japanese, he extolled the beauties of nature in a direct and modest manner. Although his earlier poems occasionally include references to classical legends or literature, late in his life he focused his attention upon what he saw and what he felt. In painting, Bōsai's most salient qualities were unworldly simplicity and inner strength. Unlike his friends Hōitsu and Bunchō, he did not paint a wide variety of subjects with great technical finesse. Instead, he depicted the serenity of the sage living within boundless nature. His landscapes are those of the scholar-artist, avoiding professional skills in order to express his personal mood and poetic spirit.

Bōsai's greatest contribution to Japanese arts may have been his calligraphy. His regular script displays a sharp angularity and strength of composition that is especially effective for inscriptions carved on stone. It was in cursive script, however, that Bōsai was most gifted. His style was based upon that of the Chinese master Huai-su, and he also absorbed some influence from the Japanese monk Ryōkan, but in his mature years Bōsai produced a large number of works that could have been brushed by no other artist. His cursive calligraphy combines exhilarating freedom with complete control of composition and brushwork. The characters twist and turn in a cosmic dance, bound together by their rhythmic flow and yet endlessly varied in shape and form. It is as though nature's own creative power flowed through his brush. Even when he was partially paralyzed in his final years, Bōsai was able to write with effortless mastery and spontaneous joy. He seems to have confidently accepted both the world around him and his own self-nature; as a result, his calligraphy is without artifice or conceit, it has simply poured forth from his own inner spirit. Viewing his works, we can understand why he was beloved not only by his friends, but by the common people of Edo.

Many aspects of Bōsai's world did not survive the generation after his death. The Meiji Restoration in 1868 led to an interest in Western, rather than Chinese, values. The Sino-Japanese War, the occupation of China and the rise of Japan as a great nation also led to a decline in interest in the philosophy and art of the literati; Bōsai was almost forgotten along with other literati painters. Because of his travels in the Niigata area, however, collectors in that region maintained an interest in Bōsai's painting and calligraphy, and a small exhibition was held in the town of Izumozaki in 1951. Nevertheless, it took the devoted efforts of Sugimura Eiji, librarian of Tokyo University, to uncover information on Bōsai's life. His book, *Kameda Bōsai*, has been the only serious publication about the artist for many years.

In recent decades there has begun a revival of appreciation for the literati aesthetic. Surprisingly enough, this has taken place as much in the Western world as in Japan. Perhaps due in part to thorough studies of Chinese literati artists, the collecting of Japanese Nanga has made great advances in the

United States, including more than one hundred examples of Bōsai's works in this country. Scholars and connoisseurs both East and West now acknowledge Bōsai as a fine poet, a painter with a unique style, and especially as one of the great cursive script calligraphers in Japanese history. Yet to see Bōsai only as an artist is to miss the true value of the man. In the literati tradition, personal character is expected to shine through all one's endeavors. Bōsai's generous and lofty spirit, accompanied by his thorough knowledge, appreciation and ability in several arts, can be communicated through time to anyone who is willing to feel the individual resonance in his poetry and brushwork.

The world of Bōsai was thus an inner world, which he shared with his friends and offered through his art to posterity. It can be intuitively appreciated by those with limited experience in painting and calligraphy as well as by experts. The sense of dancing movement in his cursive script, the enjoyment of nature and wine in his poetry and the lofty spirit of his landscapes are as fresh today as when he brushed them. This exhibition of Bōsai's work marks the first time in the West that the artistic world of an individual Japanese literatus has been fully documented. If we are willing to enter that world, we can find much to enjoy, and much to learn.

Suzuki Kiitsu, *Portrait of Bōsai*, detail

CATALOG OF WORKS IN THE EXHIBITION

1. Mitsui Shinna (1700-1782)
   Eight Immortals of the Wine-cup, 1770
   Handscroll, ink on paper, 42.2 x 673.7 cm.
   Shōka Collection

2. Inoue Kinga (1732-1784)
   Ending Aspirations and Forgetting the Self
   Hanging scroll, ink on paper, 40.3 x 65.3 cm.
   Shōka Collection

3. Inoue Kinga (1732-1784)
   Rafting Past a Mountain Village
   Hanging scroll, ink and light color on paper, 124.5 x 28.9 cm.
   Helen Foresman Spencer Museum of Art, The University of Kansas
   Gift of Dr. and Mrs. George C. Colom, 80.201

4. Inoue Kinga (1732-1784)
   Drifting in a Small Boat
   Hanging scroll, ink on paper, 66.1 x 26.2 cm.
   Mitchell Hutchinson Collection

5. Yamamoto Hokuzan (1752-1812)
   My Lazy Disposition
   Hanging scroll, ink on paper, 97 x 25 cm.
   Private Collection

6. Kameda Bōsai (1752-1826)
   Tanrakuzan, 1772
   Rubbing mounted as plaque, ink on paper, 44.5 x 101.6 cm.
   Shōka Collection

7. Kameda Bōsai (1752-1826)
   Handscroll for Yoshida Joshū's Sixtieth Birthday, 1794
   Handscroll, ink on paper, 28.2 x 205 cm.; seals 3, 9, 25
   Private Collection

8. Ike Taiga (1723-1776)
   Fishing Boat at the Reed-covered Bank
   Album leaf, ink on paper, 23 x 27.7 cm.
   The Mary and Jackson Burke Collection
   Published: Miyeko Murase, *Japanese Art: Selections from the Mary and Jackson Burke Collection* (New York, 1975), p. 246.

9. Kameda Bōsai (1752-1826)
   In the Cold River
   Album leaf, ink on paper, 23.6 x 36.2 cm.; seals 3, 19, 41
   The Mary and Jackson Burke Collection
   Published: Miyeko Murase, *Japanese Art: Selections from the Mary and Jackson Burke Collection* (New York, 1975), p. 246.

10. Kameda Bōsai (1752-1826)
    Truly a Dream, 1803
    Hanging scroll, ink and light color on paper, 55 x 130 cm.; seals 3, 25
    Cornelius and Shizuko Ouwehand Kusunoki Collection

11. Kameda Bōsai (1752-1826)
    The Ultimate Principle
    Hanging scroll, ink on paper, 96 x 27 cm.; seals 12, 20, 30
    Shōka Collection

12. Kameda Bōsai (1752-1826)
    The Virtuous Man
    Hanging scroll, ink on paper, 117.7 x 27.3 cm.; seals 6, 21, 28
    Private Collection

13. Kameda Bōsai (1752-1826)
    Eight Immortals of the Wine-cup
    Pair of six-panel screens, ink on paper, each panel 127 x 49.5 cm.; seals 43, 44
    Private Collection

14. Kameda Bōsai (1752-1826)
    Lake Mountain Scenery, 1807
    Hanging scroll, ink and light color on silk, 114.4 x 50.2 cm.; seals 3, 25, 28, 37
    Kurt and Millie Gitter Collection

15. Kameda Bōsai (1752-1826)
    A Rainbow Bridge, 1807
    Hanging scroll, ink and light color on paper, 92.7 x 33.6 cm.; seals 5, 27, 41
    Kurt and Millie Gitter Collection

16. Kameda Bōsai (1752-1826)
    Minami Sanshōki Waterfall, 1809
    Hanging scroll, ink and color on silk, 105.3 x 31 cm.; seals 3, 25
    Chien-lu Collection, Ann Arbor

17. Sō Ryōkan (1757-1831)
   Enough for a Fire
   Rubbing mounted as hanging scroll, ink on paper, 119 x 45 cm.
   Shōka Collection

18. Kameda Bōsai (1752-1826)
   The Pair of Pines, 1810
   Hanging scroll, ink on paper, 112.6 x 34 cm.; seals 3, 21, 25
   Private Collection

19. Kushiro Unsen (1759-1811)
   Viewing a Waterfall
   Hanging scroll, ink and color on paper, 118 x 40.1 cm.
   Shōka Collection

20. *Seven-String Ch'in Presented to Bōsai*, 1811
   Lacquer on wood, inlaid with mother of pearl, silk strings, 119.4 x 17.3 cm.
   Shōka Collection

21. Kameda Bōsai (1752-1826)
   Living in the Mountain Forest, 1811
   Hanging scroll, ink and color on silk, 56.3 x 79.2 cm.; seals 3, 25, 37
   Kurt and Millie Gitter Collection

22. Kameda Bōsai (1752-1826)
   Mountain Landscape
   Hanging scroll, ink and color on silk, 107 x 48.7 cm.; seals 11, 16, 27
   The Mary and Jackson Burke Collection

23. Kameda Bōsai (1752-1826)
   Old Trees
   Hanging scroll, ink on paper, 132.5 x 47 cm.; seals 10, 29, 38
   Private Collection

24. Kameda Bōsai (1752-1826)
   Growing Old
   Hanging scroll, ink on paper, 137 x 32.2 cm.; seals 10, 19, 29
   Shōka Collection

25. Signature of Kameda Bōsai
   Cursive Calligraphy
   Hanging scroll, ink on paper, 133 x 44.8 cm.; seals 16?, 31?, 42?
   Shōka Collection

26. Kameda Bōsai (1752-1826)
   Plum Villa
   Rubbing mounted as hanging scroll, ink on paper, 141 x 80.2 cm.
   Shōka Collection

27. Kameda Bōsai (1752-1826)
   Straight Trunk and Curved Branch, 1814
   Hanging scroll, ink and light color on paper, 126.5 x 30.6 cm.; seals 3, 23, 25
   Yabumoto Kōzō Collection, Japan

28. Kameda Bōsai (1752-1826)
   Kyōchūzan Album, 1816
   Five copies of woodblock printed book, ink and color on paper, 27.3 x 16.5 cm.
   Kurt and Millie Gitter, Robert Ravicz, and Shōka Collections

   28a. *Waiting for Fish in the Green Verdure*

   28b. *A Single Lake*

   28c. *Rivers and Mountains Awaken the Heart*

   28d. *Playing the Ch'in Brings Inner Harmony*

   28e. *Rivers and Mountains Rescue My Poetry*

   28f. *Green Mountains and Azure Waters*

   28g. *Yearning for a Pleasurable Place*

   28h. *Fishing Alone in the Cold River*

29. Kameda Bōsai (1752-1826)
   Alone Viewing the Cold River
   Hanging scroll, ink and light color on silk, 90.8 x 31.4 cm.; seals 10, 11
   Herbert and Sandra Burstein Collection

30. Kameda Bōsai (1752-1826)
   Bridge Between Two Cliffs
   Hanging scroll, ink and light color on paper, 68.3 x 21.6 cm.; seals 35, 37
   Dr. and Mrs. Sanford Pailet Collection

31. Signature of Kameda Bōsai
   Landscape
   Hanging scroll, ink and light color on paper, 119.4 x 31.9 cm.; seals 3?, 21?, 25?
   New Orleans Museum of Art, 82.57

32. Kameda Bōsai (1752-1826)
   Mountains in My Heart
   Hanging scroll, ink on paper, 105.4 x 30 cm.; seals 10, 29
   Mitchell Hutchinson Collection

33. Kameda Bōsai (1752-1826)
   Shirashige Shrine
   Hanging scroll, ink on silk, 100 x 27.6 cm.; seals 11, 23, 31
   Chikunai Collection

34. Kameda Bōsai (1752-1826)
   The Voice of the Cuckoo
   Fan, ink on paper, 20.5 x 43.1 cm.; seal 47
   Pine Cloud Studio Collection

35. Kameda Bōsai (1752-1826)
   Poem on Patterned Paper
   Fan, ink on paper, 17 x 46.2 cm.
   Private Collection

36. Kameda Bōsai (1752-1826)
   Forty-seven Righteous Samurai, 1819
   Rubbing mounted as hanging scroll, ink on paper, 163.7 x 87.2 cm.
   Shōka Collection

37. Illustration to the *Myōmyōkidan*, 1821
   Woodblock printed book, ink on paper, 18.4 x 12.3 cm.
   Shōka Collection

38. Kameda Bōsai (1752-1826)
   T'ang Dynasty Poems
   Six-panel screen, ink on paper, 155 x 341.6 cm.; seals 10, 11, 19, 29, 31, 42
   New Orleans Museum of Art
   Gift of Dr. and Mrs. Kurt Gitter, 79.275

39. Kameda Bōsai (1752-1826)
   Gourd, 1820
   Hanging scroll, ink on paper, 129.5 x 47 cm.
   Kurt and Millie Gitter Collection
   Published: Stephen Addiss, *Zenga and Nanga* (New Orleans, 1976), No. 50

40. Kameda Bōsai (1752-1826)
   Abalone
   Hanging scroll, ink on paper, 123.5 x 43.5 cm.; seals 10, 29, 38
   Sugimura Eiji Collection, Japan

41. Kameda Bōsai (1752-1826)
   To Know Fish
   Hanging scroll, ink on paper, 23.5 x 41.5 cm.; seals 10, 32, 42
   Danziger Collection

42. Ten Artists
   Gathered Clouds
   Hanging scroll, ink and light color on silk, 94 x 32.2 cm.; seal 45
   Pine Cloud Studio Collection

43. Six Artists
   Flowers and Poems
   Hanging scroll, ink and light color on silk, 98 x 32.7 cm.; seal 46
   Shōka Collection

44. Five Artists
   Poems on Chinese Woven Paper
   Hanging scroll, ink on woven paper with color, 106 x 43 cm.; seals 1, 2
   Private Collection

45. Kameda Bōsai (1752-1826) and Six Artists
   Six Poets
   Hanging scroll, ink and light color on silk, 120 x 66 cm.; seals 29, 31, 38
   New Orleans Museum of Art: Museum Purchase, 82.17

46. Suzuki Nanrei (1775-1844) and Kameda Bōsai (1752-1826)
   Portrait of Bashō
   Hanging scroll, ink and light color on paper, 86.7 x 27.3 cm.; seals 10, 29
   New Orleans Museum of Art: Anonymous gift, 80.181
   Published: *Japanese Paintings 1600-1900 from the New Orleans Museum of Art* (Birmingham Museum of Art, 1981), No. 36.

47. Ōnishi Keisai (dates unknown), Haruki Nanko (1759-1839) and Kameda Bōsai (1752-1826)
   Rock and Bamboo
   Hanging scroll, ink on silk, 99.2 x 29.3 cm.; seals 1, 2
   Pine Cloud Studio Collection

48. Suzuki Kiitsu (1796-1858) and Kameda Bōsai (1752-1826)
   Arrowroot
   Hanging scroll, ink and light color on paper, 99 x 29 cm.; seal 1
   Dr. and Mrs. Robert Feinberg Collection

49. Sakai Hōitsu (1761-1828) and Kameda Ryōrai (1778-1853)
   Two Warblers on a Persimmon Branch
   Hanging scroll, ink and color on silk, 140 x 51 cm.
   Dan and Carol Henderson Collection

50. Kameda Bōsai (1752-1826)
   Cliff Landscape, 1821
   Hanging scroll, ink and color on silk, 122.2 x 44.5 cm.; seals 24, 29, 31
   Kurt and Millie Gitter Collection
   Published: *Kokka* No. 441
   I'izuka Bei'u, *Nihonga taisei* (Tokyo, 1931-34), vol. 10, pl. 56
   Stephen Addiss, *Zenga and Nanga* (New Orleans, 1976), No. 49

51. Kameda Bōsai (1752-1826)
   Mountain Colors
   Hanging scroll, ink and color on stain, 117.4 x 45.1 cm.; seals 24, 31, 33
   Betsy and Karel Reisz Collection, London

52. Kuwagata Keisai (1764-1824)
   Illustration to *Ryōri tsū*
   Woodblock printed book, ink on paper, 15.2 x 21.4 cm.
   Robert Ravicz Collection

53. Kameda Bōsai (1752-1826)
   In My Leisure, 1823
   Fan, ink and color on paper, 18.2 x 50 cm.; seals 12, 23, 46
   Private Collection

54. Kameda Bōsai (1752-1826), Tani Bunchō (1763-1840), and Sakai Hōitsu (1761-1828)
   Shibaraku, 1823
   Hanging scroll, ink and light color on satin, 103.5 x 45.3 cm.; seal 17
   Museum Reitburg Zurich, Collection Heinz Brasch
   Donated by Balthasar Reinhart, Winterthur

55. Tsunoda Kunisada (1786-1864)
   Danjurō in Shibaraku, 1852
   Woodblock print, ink and color on paper, 36.5 x 25.7 cm.
   Stuart Jackson Gallery, Toronto

56. Kameda Bōsai (1752-1826)
   Kotobuki, 1823
   Hanging scroll, ink on silk, 57.4 x 64.5 cm.; seals 16, 24, 31
   Private Collection

57. Kameda Bōsai (1752-1826)
   Monkey, 1824
   Hanging scroll, ink and light color on paper, 127 x 29.2 cm.; seals 4, 11, 24, 29, 31, 32, 41, 42
   Jay L. Federman, M.D. Collection

58. Suzuki Kiitsu (1796-1858)
   Portrait of Bōsai
   Hanging scroll, ink and color on silk, 89.8 x 41.6 cm.
   Kameda Toyoji Collection, Japan

59. Kameda Bōsai (1752-1826)
   Landscape [color added by Tani Bunchō (1763-1840) in 1838]
   Hanging scroll, ink and light color on paper, 27.9 x 45.1 cm.; seals 32, 45
   Keigensai Collection

60. Kameda Ryōrai (1778-1853)
   Black Kites Fly
   Hanging scroll, ink on paper, 101 x 25.5 cm.
   Private Collection

61. Kameda Ryōrai (1778-1853)
   My Family Heritage, 1847
   Hanging scroll, ink on silk, 99.7 x 66 cm.
   Prudence Myer Collection

62. Maki Ryōkō (1777-1843)
   Clear, Empty and Bright
   Hanging scroll, ink on paper, 44.1 x 29.2 cm.
   Private Collection

63. Maki Ryōkō (1777-1843)
   Tea Song
   Hanging scroll, ink on silk, 37.5 x 51.3 cm.
   Shōka Collection

SELECTED BIBLIOGRAPHY OF PUBLICATIONS BY OR CONCERNING KAMEDA BŌSAI

Kameda Bōsai. *Bussetsu maka shubutsu myōraku kyō* (Sutra of the Great Vision of Exquisite Pleasure of the Wine Buddha, Edo, 1823).

Kameda Bōsai. *Daigaku shikō* (A Personal Interpretation of the "Great Learning," Edo, 1799).

Kameda Bōsai. "Fukoku zatsugi" (Miscellaneous Rules on Natural Resources) [1781] Published in *Nihon keizai sōsho* (Japanese Economic Series), Vol. 19 (Tokyo, 1915).

Kameda Bōsai. *Kōsei ichiren* (One View from Kōsei) [a five-volume study of etymology] (Edo, 1842).

Kameda Bōsai. *Kyōchūzan* (Mountains in My Heart, Edo, 1816).

Kameda Bōsai. *Kyūchū mōkyō* (Searching Through Ancient Writings [1800] Sado, 1814).

Kameda Bōsai. *Rongo sakkai* (Explanations of the Analects) [1779]. Included in *Zenshindo ikkagen* (Edo, 1823).

Kameda Bōsai. *Shoshoku tōryō ben* (Analysis of Grains [1798] Sado, 1805).

Kameda Bōsai. *Zenshindō ikkagen* (A Personal View from Zenshindō, Edo, 1823).

Addiss, Stephen. *Nanga Paintings* (London, 1975).

Addiss, Stephen. *Zenga and Nanga; Paintings by Japanese Monks and Scholars from the Collection of Kurt and Millie Gitter* (New Orleans, 1976).

Addiss, Stephen. "Kameda Bōsai," *Enclycopedia of Japan* (New York, 1983).

Addiss, Stephen. "The Literati Paintings of Kameda Bōsai," *Chūgoku koten kenkyū* (The Journal of Sinology, Tokyo, in press).

Addiss, Stephen, et. al., *Japanese Paintings 1600-1900 from the New Orleans Museum of Art* (Birmingham, Alabama, 1982).

Addiss, Stephen, et. al., *A Myriad of Autumn Leaves: Japanese Art from the Kurt and Millie Gitter Collection* (New Orleans, 1983).

Addiss, Stephen, ed. *Bōsai Society Newsletter* Nos. 1-6 (Lawrence, Kansas, 1979-1983).

Agawa Masamichi. "Kameda Bōsai no 'Unsen Sanjin bomei' yakuchū" (Transcription and Notes on Kameda Bōsai's "Unsen's Epitaph"), *Chūgoku koten kenkyū* (The Journal of Sinology), No. 26 (Tokyo, 1981).

Aikawa Shiga. "Bōsai Sengakuji no gishi hi" (The Memorial Stone at Sengakuji with Text by Bōsai), *Kōzuke oyobi Kōzukejin* (Kōzuke and People of Kōzuke), No. 12 (October, 1925).

Aoyagi Tōri. *Zokushoka jinbusshi* (Continuing Records of Scholars, Edo, 1829).

Bokubi (Ink Beauty), No. 148 (Kyoto, 1965) and No. 181 (Kyoto, 1968).

Bokuseki Bunjinga Rimpa meihinten (Ink Traces: Literati and Rimpa Painting Exhibition, Tokyo, 1980).

"Bōsai no ihitsu takuhon ni" (Regarding Rubbings of Bōsai's Calligraphy). *Jōmō Shinbun* (July 3, 1981).

"Bōsai no kaisho hi" (Bōsai's Regular Script Memorial Stone), *Shodō*, Vol. 12, No. 6 (June, 1943).

Dai-ichi Shuppan Center, ed. *Nihon shodō taikei* (The Lineage of Japanese Calligraphy), Vol. 7 (Tokyo, 1972).

Dawes, Leonard G. *Japanese Illustrated Books* (London, 1972).

Furukawa Osamu. "Kameda Bōsai no e ni tsuite" (Regarding Kameda Bōsai's Paintings), *Shoga kottō zasshi*, No. 285 (Tokyo, 1932).

Furukawa Osamu. "Kameda Bōsai o ronzu" (Discussing Kameda Bōsai), *Daitō geijutsu*, Vol. 1, Nos. 2-7 (1930).

Furukawa Osamu. "Kameda Bōsai to Kushiro Unsen," *Shoga kottō zasshi*, No. 358 (April, 1938).

Gumma no Nihonga ten (Japanese Painting Exhibition in Gumma, 1976).

Harada Kampei. "Bōsai to Ryōkan," *Bokubi*, No. 148 (Kyoto, 1965).

Harada Kampei. "Kameda Bōsai ryakuden" (An Abridged Life of Kameda Bōsai), *Bokubi*, No. 148 (Kyoto, 1965).

Haruna Yoshie. *Nihon shodōshi* (A History of Japanese Calligraphy, Kyoto, 1974).

Hasegawa Ryōzō. "Kameda Bōsai no kin" (Kameda Bōsai's Ch'in), *Shoga kottō zasshi*, No. 278 (1931).

Hida Akimitsu. "Sugimura Eiji cho 'Kameda Bōsai' " (A review of Sugimura Eiji's "Kameda Bōsai"), *Kokuhō to kokubungaku* (National Law and Literature, Tokyo, 1979).

Higashi Kan'ichi. "Kameda Bōsai," *Kinsei hyaku ketsuden* (Tokyo, 1954).

Hillier, Jack and Smith, Lawrence. *Japanese Prints: 300 Years of Albums and Books* (London, 1980).

Holloway, Owen E. *Graphic Art of Japan* (London, 1957).

Ihara Kun'ichi. "Chazan Bōsai Nihonbashi kaizōzu ni tsuite" (Regarding a Painting of the Chance Meeting of Chazan and Bōsai at Nihonbashi). *Bingo shidan*, Vol. 1, No. 3 (1925) and Vol. 2, No. 11 (1926).

Inoue Kinga. *Kinga Sensei keigi setchū* (Kinga's Philosophical Eclecticism, Edo, 1764).

"Kameda Bōsai," *Kensei bijutsu*, No. 134 (Tokyo, 1919).

"Kameda Bōsai hitsu shūkei sansui zukai" (Regarding Kameda Bōsai's "Autumn Landscape"), *Kokka*, No. 441 (Tokyo, 1928).

"Kameda Bōsai Sensei," *Kyōdo no hana* (Flowers of our Birthplace, Tōsei Elementary School, Tokyo, 1918).

"Kameda Bōsai shinnen shokan" (A Short New Year's Letter by Kameda Bōsai), *Sho-en*, Vol. 7, No. 3 (January, 1917).

"Kameda Bōsai shinseki shin baisō hiki" (The True Autograph of the New Plum Villa Monument Manuscript), *Sho-en*, Vol. 5, No. 2 (April, 1915).

Kameda Unbō. "Bōsai to Ryōkan to Bunchō" (Bōsai, Ryōkan and Bunchō), *Shinbijutsu*, Vol. 2, No. 5 (Tokyo, 1918).

Kanda Kichijirō et. al., eds. *Shodō zenshū* (A Complete Collection of Calligraphy), Vol. 23 (Tokyo, 1958).

Kantō bunjinga (Literati Painting of the Kantō Area, Niigata, 1971).

Katō Yoshikazu. "Ryōkan to Kameda Bōsai," *Mainichi Shinbun* and *Niigata Nippo* (Niigata Daily News), (Both January 4th 1982).

Kayahara Tōgaku. "Sumidagawa ni okeru Kameda Bōsai no nishihi" (Two Stone Monuments Engraved with Poems by Kameda Bōsai Along the Sumida River), *Shoga-en*, Nos. 1-2 (Tokyo, 1924).

Kayahara Tōgaku. "Sumidagawa-ue ni okeru Bōsai no nishihi" (Two Stone Monuments Engraved with Poems by Bōsai Along the Sumida River), *Nihon bijutsu*, No. 16 (April, 1930).

"Kokusaiteki na Ryōkan-sama aitsugu gaikoku no okyaku-sama" (A Foreign Guest Visits the Home of Ryōkan), *Ryōkan*, Vol. 5 (Niigata, November, 1981).

Mitamura Genryū. "Akō yonjūshichi gishi to Bōsai Sensei" (The Forty-Seven Righteous Samurai of Akō and Bōsai), *Nihon oyobi Nihonjin* (Japan and the People of Japan), No. 531 (1910).

Mitchell, Charles. *Biobibliography of Nanga, Maruyama and Shijō Illustrated Books* (Los Angeles, 1972).

Murase Miyeko. *Japanese Art: Selections from the Mary and Jackson Burke Collection* (New York, 1975).

Murayama Furusato. "Igai na ikku" (Unusual Haiku), *Taiyō* (Autumn, 1976).

Murayama Yoshihiro. "Kameda Bōsai no 'Unsen Sanjin bomei' ni tsuite" (Regarding Kameda Bōsai's Unsen's Epitaph"), *Chūgoku koten kenkyū* (The Journal of Sinology), No. 26 (Tokyo, 1981).

Nakajima Buzan. "Zōtei Kameda san sensei denjitsu" (Augmented and Corrected, Three Kameda Masters: A True Private Record), *Sho-en*, Vol. 6, Nos. 4-10 (Tokyo, 1942).

Nakajima Keitarō. *Kameda san sensei denjitsu shiki* (Three Kameda Masters: A True Private Record) [1889] Published in Sugimura, *Kameda Bōsai* (Tokyo, 1979).

Nakamura Shin'ichirō. "Kokugaku to Kangaku no Edo-ryū" (The Edo school of Chinese and Japanese Studies), *Mainichi Shinbun* (January 5, 1979).

Nakane Kōtei. *Kōtei gadan* (Elegant Discussions by Kōtei, Tokyo, 1886).

Nihonga taisei (Comprehensive Illustrated Survey of Japanese Painting), Vol. 10 (Tokyo, 1930).

Nishikawa Gyokko. "Bōsai Sensei itsuji" (Anecdotes about Bōsai), *Kōzuke oyobi Kōzukejin*, Nos. 82-84 (Feb.-April, 1924).

Nishikawa Gyokko. "Kameda Bōsai Sensei den" (The Life of Kameda Bōsai), *Kōzuke oyobi Kōzukejin*, Nos. 77, 79 (1923).

Nishina Hakkoku, ed. *Bōsai Sensei bunshō* (Selected Prose of Bōsai, Edo, 1828).

Nishina Hakkoku, ed. *Bōsai Sensei shishō* (A Selection of Bōsai's Poems, Edo, 1822).

Saitō Shiseki. "Kameda Bōsai to Saitama bunka" (Kameda Bōsai and Saitama Culture), *Musashino shidan*, Vol. 2, Nos. 3-4 (Feb.-March, 1953).

Sakamoto Tarō, et. al., eds. *Sho no Nihonshi* (Japan's Calligraphic History), Vol. 6 (Tokyo, 1975).

Satō Ungai. "Gyosho mandan" (A Fisherman's Book of Idle Talk), *Kōzuke oyobi Kōzukejin*, No. 168 (1931).

Sekigushi Rō-un. "Kameda Bōsai," *Nanshū gashi*, No. 1 (1900).

Shimpen Saitama kenshi (New Compilation of Saitama Prefecture History), Shiryō hen 12, Kinsei 3, Bunka (Tokyo, 1982).

Sōma Zaifū. *Taigu Ryōkan* (Tokyo, 1918).

Sorimachi Shigeo. *Catalogue of Japanese Illustrated Books and Manuscripts in the Spencer Collection of the New York Public Library* (Tokyo, 1978).

Sugimura Eiji. *Kameda Bōsai* (Tokyo, 1979).

Sugimura Eiji. "Kameda Bōsai yowa" (Further Discussion of Kameda Bōsai), *Tokyo Daigaku U. P.* (Tokyo "University Press"), Vol. 10, No. 10 (October, 1981).

Sugimura Eiji. "Kameda Bōsai yowa" (Further Discussion of Kameda Bōsai), *Kiden*, No. 6 (Tokyo, November, 1982).

Sugimura Eiji, ed. *Kameda Bōsai shibun-shoga shū* (Collection of Bōsai's Prose, Poetry, Calligraphy and Painting, Tokyo, 1982).

Toda Kenji. *The Ryerson Collection of Japanese and Chinese Illustrated Books* (Chicago, 1931).

Togari Soshin'an. "Ryōkan no sho to Bōsai soshite kaisō" (Ryōkan's Calligraphy and Bōsai: Expressions of the Heart), *Atorie*, Vol. 15, No. 8 (June, 1938).

Tō Isei. "Bōsai jobun Hōitsu mosha Kōrin gashū reihon ni sesshite" (Regarding Bōsai's Introduction to Hōitsu's Volume of Kōrin Paintings), *Hondōraku*, Vol. 1, No. 6 (1926).

Udaka Ōha. "Shokuzan, Bōsai to Kōyō tōinkan" (Shokusanjin, Bōsai and the Kōyō Drinking Contest Scroll), *Fude no tomo* (Friend of the Brush), No. 248 (1921).

Umezawa Sei-ichi. *Nihon Nanga shi* (A History of Japanese Nanga, Tokyo, 1919).

Watanabe Chisui. "Kameda Bōsai to Nishina Hakkoku," *Shoga kottō zasshi*, No. 277 (1931).

Yamamoto Shūnosuke. *Kameda Bōsai shōden* (A Short Life of Kameda Bōsai, Niigata, 1951).

Yamamoto Shūnosuke. "Kameda Bōsai no Sado jin'en shokan" (Kameda Bōsai's Letters to Friends on Sado Island), *Sado shigaku*, Nos. 1-4, 7 (Sado, 1959-1971).

Yamamoto Shūnosuke. "Kameda Bōsai no Echigo jin'en shokan" (Kameda Bōsai's Letters to Friends in Echigo), *Echisa kenkyū*, No. 29 (Niigata, 1970).

Yamanouchi Chōzō. *Nihon Nanga shi* (A History of Japanese Nanga, Tokyo, 1981).

Yamashita Shigeru. "Bōsai Sensei no bokuseki" (Bōsai's Ink Traces), *Shoga sōdan* (Discussions of Calligraphy and Painting), Vol. 4, Nos. 3-4 (March-April, 1920).

Yokoyama Kendō. "Sakurabana gakka gojūsan tsugi" (Cherry Blossoms, Painters and the Fifty-Three Stations of the Tōkaidō), *Nihon oyobi Nihonjin*, No. 579 (April, 1912).

Yoshino Sei-iku. "Bōsai Kameda Sensei den" (The Life of Kameda Bōsai), *Kinryō ikō*, Vol. 7 (Tokyo, 1888).

Young, Martie. *Asian Art: A Collector's Selection* (Ithaca, New York, 1973).

Appendix A:
TRANSLATIONS OF JAPANESE TEXTS

1. Text to Catalog Nos. 1 and 13.

EIGHT IMMORTALS OF THE WINE-CUP (Attributed to Tu Fu)

Ho Chih-chang rides his horse
    as though he were on a swaying ship;
If bleary-eyed he should tumble down a well,
    he would lie at the bottom, fast asleep.

Prince Ju-yang drinks three measures
    before going to court;
If he passes a brewer's cart along the way,
    his mouth waters—
He regrets only
    that he is not the Prince of Wine Springs.

The Minister of the left
    spends ten thousand coins daily,
Drinking like a whale,
    imbibing like one hundred rivers,
Holding his wine cup, he insists
    "I drink as a sage and avoid virtue."

Ts'ui Tsung-chih, a handsome youth,
    is exceedingly refined;
Turning his gaze to the heavens
    and grasping his beloved cup,
He stands like a tree of jade,
    swaying lightly in the breeze.

The ascetic Su Chin meditates
    before an embroidered scroll of the Buddha,
But he enjoys his lapses
    when he goes off on a spree.

As for Li Po, one measure
    will inspire one hundred poems;
He sleeps in the wine-shops
    of the capital, Ch'ang An,
And when summoned by the Emperor,
    will not board the Imperial barge;
He calls himself "The official
    who is the god of wine."

Give three cupfulls to the calligrapher Chang Hsu
    and his writing becomes inspired—
He throws off his cap before the officials,
    and his brush produces clouds and mist.
After five measures, Chiao Sui is so eloquent
    that he startles everyone in the feasting hall.

2. Text to Catalog No. 7.

PREFACE PRESENTED TO MASTER YOSHIDA JOSHŪ
ON THE OCCASION OF HIS SIXTIETH BIRTHDAY

When men obtain Heaven-bestowed fortune, there is always a reason for it; human strength alone cannot bring it about. There are four kinds of Heaven-bestowed fortune. One is called "wordly fortune," which refers to families with present official employment. The second is called "never fading," which refers to one's fame and reputation being transmitted through the generations. The third is called "carrying on the fine (tradition)," which means that when there is superior virtue in one generation, the later generations can keep alive the desire to do good. The fourth is called "longevity," which refers to such figures as [the semi-legendary Chinese and Japanese ministers] Tung-fang Shuo and Takeuchi Nosukune.

When the Divine Imperial Ancestor (Japan's first "historical" Emperor Jimmu) in accordance with Heavenly Will received the transmission and governed over the realm, by which time there had been two hundred years of peaceful government, there existed all kinds of men, be they military leaders, ministers, wise counselors, medical practitioners or diviners —all with special talents who obtained official positions. These were cases of "worldly fortune." Those among them whose "fame and reputation were transmitted through generations" enjoyed this fate because of qualities innate within them, and this can be said to be a rare thing. As for "continuing to keep alive the desire to do good," there are few such men in the world, and it can be said to be still more difficult. At the present time, those who combine these three things are rare indeed. Of men I myself have known, there is perhaps only one, Yoshida Joshū.

If we trace his origins, we find that the Master came from the line of the Imperial Prince Atsutane, son of Emperor Uda (reigned 887-897). The distant descendent of this Prince, Mitsuhide, was a man whose nature it was to love the art of medicine. He called himself Jin'an and served as physician-in-waiting to the Muromachi Shogun.[1] He was officially given a fief of his own, and his family received an inheritable emolument as doctors. This continued through the Muromachi period and the period of Toyotomi (Hideyoshi, 1536-1598) into the current period, being transmitted now for several tens of generations. In every generation, the family has controlled the position of Physician General, and has been known as one of the Four Great Schools of Medicine. Indeed, it has been one of the distinguished clans of the Kantō region. This can be called a supreme example of "worldly fortune."

Jin'an's great-grandson, Master Jikka, because of his skill was sent west to accompany the ambassador to Ming dynasty China. None of the Chinese doctors was able to surpass him. When faced with medical predicaments, he applied his techniques and brought the (all but) dead back to life as if by divine power. At this, the Chinese shouted his praises, ten thousand people crying out with one voice along the roads. They named him "The I-an" (Hermitage of Thought) of Japan, adopting a phrase it is said from Hsu Yin-tsung (a great physician of the T'ang dynasty who is supposed to have claimed that "medicine is a matter of thought"). A famous man of the Ming dynasty, Fang Mei-ya[2] wrote out the two large characters Ch'eng-i (In accord with thought) and presented them to Jikka. Needless to say, the Master changed his previous name and now called himself "I-an."

During a second trip to China, it happened that the Emperor Shih-tsung Su Huang-ti (the Chiaching Emperor, r. 1522-1566) became ill. All the native doctors folded their arms (and gave up), but the Emperor heard about Master I-an. He ordered him to treat the illness; just one dose of I-an's "life medicine" and the Emperor immediately arose in good health. Thereupon I-an was presented with gifts on several occasions, and sent home robed in silk. The copy of the Sheng-chi tsung-lu (tsuan-yao) (A Compendium of Sagely Remedies),[3] the portrait of Pien Ch'ueh (a famous legendary physician) by Yen Hui (the great Yuan dynasty figure painter), the medicine chest and the fine inks— all in his family collection—were presented to him by the Emperor. Thus the Master's fame was great in a foreign land; this can be considered a supreme example of "never fading."

The Master's son also used the name I-an.[4] During the Keichō period (1596-1611) the Emperor Go-yōzei contracted an unusual disease, so he summoned this Master and ordered him to carry out an examination. The Master prescribed a medicine, after which the illness immediately was cured. The Emperor serenely took on a calm expression and, greatly pleased, said "The illness came with a life of its own, but you responded to it with composure. With such a sharp ax in hand, what do intertwined roots mean to you? From now on, you can use the name 'Composure in Accord with Thought.'"

This Master I-an wrote Books on Medicine in eight sections and one hundred and several tens of volumes, all constituting key works in the field. This can be called a supreme example of "carrying on the fine (tradition)."

Ah! Joshū's family in past generations having thus repeatedly produced famous men, it is especially difficult for the present holder of the name to follow in their footsteps. The current Master occupying this difficult position has exerted himself to the utmost to implement humaneness, and yet he still has considered his own efforts to be inadequate. His noble son Chimon,[5] with his talent that sets a standard for past and present, continues the enterprise; he is a man of sincerity and kindness, in no particular out of step with his ancestors. How could he not continue along the glorious path of previous generations?

The Master is now sixty years old. His hearing and sight are as good as always; a lustre still shows in his hair. These are the benefits of the secret techniques for nurturing inner vitality and extending longevity, as well as the alchemical recipes for elixir, all of which have been transmitted in his family. Hence it is needless to say that the reckoning of his years will be as mountains, and his health will be as evergreens. This can be considered a supreme example of longevity.

Today on the twenty-sixth day of the eleventh month of the year kō-in (1794), it is the Master's date of passage, so a great celebration is being given to congratulate him. We will all "ascend to the common hall" to drink to his possessing "The Three Manys,"[6] and to sing to him the poem of "Nine Likes,"[7] all joyfully engaging in happy activities.

The Master has requested that I write something for him, so rather than desisting on the grounds of my inferior ability, I have sketched the general picture as above. The Master said "You praise the virtues of my ancestors so as to congratulate me, and that would have been sufficient. When you extoll me for 'exerting myself to the utmost to implement humaneness', however, I feel unworthy of such praise."

I replied, "Sir, do not be so humble! The task of maintaining the glorious tradition of several tens of generations of great men cannot be accomplished unless one 'exerts oneself to the utmost!' Moreover, Sir, your family has produced over ten generations of physicians. From the Emperor of a foreign land to the common people, how many thousands of dying people have they brought back to health! You, Sir, have continued this traditional trade, and have passed it down to the next generation—these marvelous techniques which, once applied, bring the [all but] dead back to life—and those who have benefited from your beneficence have not been few. Hence your humaneness is apparent. Confucius said 'The humane man will live long.' Hence it can be seen, Sir, that your enjoyment of longevity derives from your humaneness. It is because of this that I have extolled you. I would hope that these comments differ from the shallow words usually presented on holidays."

Upon hearing this, the Master smiled happily and said "Indeed, this is good praise and good felicitation! May it be passed on to my sons and grandsons so they may peruse its words!"[8]

> —Twenty-sixth day of the second winter month,
> the year kō-in [1794],
> Kameda Bōsai presents this
> bowing his head and prostrating himself
> twice.

3. Bōsai's Preface to Hōitsu's *Kōrin hyakuzu* (One Hundred Paintings of Kōrin).

Ōgata Kōrin was good at painting. He escaped from the narrow confines of the academic style and put forth a style of his own. In portraits, he revealed the inner nature with his brush. In insects and flowers, he imbued the paper with feeling. His painting style was uncommon; his spirit resonance was exalted. Hence he stood supreme in his time, and was dubbed "Divinely Untrammeled." There were no later men who could follow in his footsteps. Only the monk Hōitsu was able to master his style of brushwork and achieve a similar high degree of refinement.

The second day of the sixth month of the twelfth year of Bunka [1815] marked the centenary of Kōrin's death. Hōitsu gathered together the cultivated men of our day, and humbly undertook to organize a memorial celebration. He collected works by Kōrin from collections near and far, making copies of each work as he received it, ultimately obtaining a total of one hundred pictures. He then made additional, reduced copies and had them printed so that they could be transmitted in the world.

Ah! This action alone suffices to reveal the sincerity of Hōitsu's love. If the dead have consciousness, Kōrin must consider Hōitsu to be the kind of friend one wants to spend mornings and evenings with.[9]

> —Written by Kameda Bōsai Kō

4. Text to Catalog No. 26.

A RECORD OF THE PLUM VILLA AT INK-TEAR POND

By the banks of Ink-Tear pond, alongside Vine Slope, an overgrown garden has been cultivated anew. Gazing at it, one sees a view like white waves curling against the sky, or like the silver towers of the P'eng-lai paradise, unapproachable beneath the sea. It is like the fine jade at Lan-t'ien Fields cropping up in clusters, producing mist. Perhaps this is what Su Shih meant by "flowers like an ocean."

One must laugh at Yuan Feng, "lifting the curtain and stuffing the stove," and also wonder at Ta-yu Ridge's reputation for being one of the world's great spots for plum trees when there were actually only thirty of them planted there!

The master of this villa, Kikuyu, is a rare gentleman, a man of fine taste and spirit. Ten years have passed since he first planted plum trees, and they have now become one of the most magnificent sights of the capital. Wealthy landowners, rich householders, reclusive men of subtle sensibility and afficionados of fine things all visit this place, bringing wine-jars with them. I too have come several times to see the plums.

This spring, I wanted to see them both opening and withering—to observe their entire cycle of beginning, flourishing and fading. I therefore came to observe the blossoms here on snowy days, moonlit nights, rainy mornings, windy evenings, in weather clear and bright or cloudy and obscure, in dawn sunlight or dusk sunset, and I exhaustively examined each and every one of the flowers' manifestations and moods: happy or angry, asleep or awake.

One evening in the moonlight, I was enjoying the flowers while drinking wine. I became intoxicated, and lay down to sleep. Suddenly, there appeared in a dream a large woman who called herself "The Flower Maiden." She approached, leading a retinue of one hundred beautiful women. Their white silk-sleeved robes were all uniform, their make-up was also the same. It was like a descent of Indra's bevy of beautiful women at the city of Vaisali.[10] As I looked all about me, I saw that their flesh was translucent, like ice, and their bones crystalline, like jade. Their deportment was refined, exalted—all of them had the demeanor of immortals. Truly, these were beauties from beyond the ordinary world. The Flower Maiden said to me, "In former times, Lu Fang-weng[11] loved hai-t'ang blossoms, and dubbed himself 'The Hai-t'ang Crazy.' Now you, Sir, deeply love plum blossoms, so I declare you to be 'The Plum Blossom Crazy.' For the hai-t'ang blossom has a sensuous beauty, while the plum blossom has a pure beauty. If we can compare being crazy about purity with being crazy about sensuousness, the craziness may be the same, but the taste is different. As for your craziness, sir, I can see the purity in it." With this, she bade one beauty offer me a goblet and urged me to drink from it. When I did so, I instantly sensed that my body had taken on a fragrance and a lightness. Then there was a coughing sound at my pillow; I abruptly awoke and looked around. No one was there. All I could see was the master of the villa reading through Mr. Fan's *Encyclopedia of Plum Blossoms* and writing annotations in it. He turned to me and said "Have you seen a ghost? Why were you moaning and groaning like that?" I told him what I had seen in my dream, and also told him it was appropriate for him, the master of the villa, to be given the name of "Plum Blossom Crazy"—a man of common substance such as myself was unworthy of it. I then wrote these words down, and departed.[12]

—Eleventh year of Bunka [1814] Spring,
second month, fifteenth day.

5. Text to Catalog No. 36.

STELE INSCRIPTION FOR THE FORTY-SEVEN RIGHTEOUS SAMURAI OF AKŌ

Moral heroism derives from inner sincerity, and can move Heaven and earth and cause feelings in the gods; the noble actions it gives rise to awesomely constitute a standard for loyal subjects over a hundred generations. Hence this heroism can help to correct shallow customs and reinvigorate the samurai spirit.

During the Genroku era [1688-1703] the then *daimyō* of Akō, resenting Lord Kira's arrogance, stabbed him in the Imperial Palace but failed to kill him. He thus committed the crime of disrespect for the court, and was commanded to die; he was also dispossessed of his fief. Because this event was unforeseen, all the subjects of the *daimyō* became anxious, not knowing what to do. There was agitated debate, as everyone was uneasy at heart. Some equivocated and found it impossible to rouse themselves to action: they folded their arms and lost heart. After a time, considering their overall situation, they decided to take an oath to "cast off the old and seek something new," so they fled, taking their families with them.

As for those who were impatient and impulsive, and who thus failed to remain faithful to real moral commitment, they grandiosely grasped their wrists and vowed to hold the castle and refuse to surrender to the court's orders, and to remain there unto the point of dying together with their lord. They failed to realize that they were thus damaging the proper relationship between lord and subject, as well as defying the law of the land; on the contrary, they were adding to the seriousness of their late lord's offence!

Yoshio had been a retainer of Akō for a long time. Calmly, he opposed the various suggested courses of action; adhering to proper form, he complied with the law, surrendered the castle, and departed from it. For his ultimate purpose was to revenge his late lord.

He thereupon assembled forty-six men of determination who had been retainers in the fief, took leadership upon himself, and strengthened the men's resolve. According to plan, they then divided into groups, and one night secretly entered the estate of Lord Kira, where they assassinated him with a single blow. Thus, they instantly cleansed the wrong done to their late lord in the Ninefold Springs of the underworld. But because they had "mobilized a mob and sent forth troops at night in the capital," the government, in accordance with its laws, ordered each of them to die.

The Sengakuji was a temple which had benefited from donations by the *daimyō*. The abbot, Master On, made a request to obtain the bodies and was granted permission to bury them around the tomb of their late lord. He then erected an inscription which read "Tombs of the Forty-Seven Righteous Samurai." Ah, is it possible that Master On himself was a "righteous samurai!" Everyone who came to visit these tombs would linger and sigh, and would find it difficult to pull himself away.

It is now over a hundred years since then, and people still think admiringly of these men as though only one day has passed. Even ordinary men, women and children can recite their names, and, moved by their actions, weep tears and praise them ceaselessly. Such is the extent to which their moral heroism, which derived from their inner sincerity, has moved Heaven and Earth and caused feelings in the gods, awesomely inspiring a thousand generations, and brilliantly enduring, indestructible, together with the universe.

Moreover, Yoshio, taking the initiative in this righteous action, successfully concealed his true intentions, and never leaked his plans; he experienced great hardships, but never slackened in his determination. Prior to executing his plan he spied on his enemies, who were carefully watching for expressions of worry or suspiciousness on his part. He indulged in a life of drinking and associating with geisha in order to relieve Kira's anxiety and put him off guard. The painstaking thoroughness of his concept could not be achieved in one day alone! In addition, he persuaded the other forty-six men to accept his authority and follow his orders, and to achieve their goal successfully in one move: from these things it can be seen that his superior ability was sufficient to the purpose of carrying out this strategy, and his intelligence sufficient to act at the right moment. Hence the reason the noble action from beginning to end was unified and not fragmented, and shines brilliantly, unique in a thousand generations.

Ah! Who is there who does not possess a human heart imbued with Heavenly Principle? And if a man has a human heart, how can he not admire their spirit and empathize with their determination? Whenever I hear about this affair of the retainers of Akō, I am always moved, and I grasp my wrist and weep tears! And yet at that time, in discussions about the affair, there were those who stupidly fabricated idiosyncratic opinions and twisted theories, taking it upon themselves to give willful interpretations of the incident. The extreme ones even went so far as to misuse the historiographical methods of the *Spring and Autumn Annals,*[13] using the term "rebel" to describe the righteous samurai! This must have been either because these men were jealous of the great virtue of [the *rōnin's*] loyal spirit, or because the human heart imbued with Heavenly Principle had been extinguished in them. This was essentially a matter of traitorous officials and petty-minded men using sophistry to injure the good. Must they not tremble in fear at having thus incurred the wrath of godmen?

It is respectfully considered that this heart-inspired affair of Yoshio and the other forty-six men is like the sun in the sky, and their magnificent moral energy can still awesomely invigorate the spirit of righteousness in the world and inspire the spirit of the samurai of the world. Is not its relevance to moral education in society extremely great?

The present abbot of Sengakuji, Master Kin, greatly turning the wheel of Dharma and vastly disseminating the influence of his sect, has now remained faithful to the intentions of the former abbot, Master On, by honoring the tombs of the righteous samurai. Hence he has asked me to compose a text to be engraved in stone and erected beside the tombs. Ah, is it possible that Master Kin is also a righteous samurai?[14]

> —*Bunsei second year [1819], the third month of spring, composed and written by Kameda Kō of Edo*
>
> —*Engraved by Hirose Muretazu*

6. Bōsai's Preface to *Gyōsho ruisan* (An Encyclopedic Compilation of Running Script).

Seal, clerical, running and cursive scripts are different types of writing; running script can encompass clerical and cursive. If, however, one writes running script on the basis of clerical, it will be too constricted; if on the basis of cursive, too loose. If one parts from squareness and follows roundness, striking a balance between heavy and fine, and is in accord with the proper measure of downward and upward movement, then it will be like winds blowing and rain falling, rich in lustre with opening blossoms, but with a touch of sad, autumnal elegance; this is to master the running style. Seki Kokumei is the grandson of Hōkō and the son of Nan'rō (Kinui). For these three generations, the glorious tradition has been continued; holding the brush and working at calligraphy, all three men have soared together through the world. For this reason they have collected in their home no less than 500 works of calligraphy and old rubbings. How elegant and flourishing! Kokumei once said "There have been collected volumes on clerical and cursive scripts of past and present [examples are cited]. All of these are excellent and worth reading. But in the case of running script alone I have never heard of a book being compiled. Why is this? It has indeed been a lack in the Garden of Art, and a cause for lingering regret on the part of calligraphers."

He thereupon perused all books on calligraphy, past and present, and gathered together reliable examples. He examined them all, selecting the finest masterpieces to create *Gyōsho ruisan,* a generous and rich sampling to which he has devoted much effort. Herein can be seen the extent of his family's learning.

Running script styles are extremely varied; if one does not profusely penetrate them all and select models amongst them, one cannot comprehend the stylistic resonances of the great masters. Beginning students need only study from this book. They must realize that it first derives from the styles of the Han and Wei dynasties, and secondly it does not fail to include the forms of Chin and T'ang. However, it does avoid the vulgar practices of later periods, such as static thickness and gross coarseness. As for the *Lan-t'ing* and the *Sheng-chiao* [showing the calligraphy of Wang Hsi-chih] and the works of Yen Chen-ch'ing, their heavenly excellence is brilliant beyond description. They are the examples from which one must work.[15]

—Winter, eleventh month of the second year of Bunsei [1819]

7. Bōsai's Sutra: The Great Vision of Exquisite Pleasure of the Wine Buddha.

BUSSETSU MAKA SHUBUTSU MYŌRAKU KYŌ

The Japanese Buddhist follower Bōsai Kō explains what he has heard: Once, the Buddha was at Enjoy-Drinking-No-Regrets Mountain, with the Seven Sages of the Bamboo Grove and the Eight Immortals of the Wine Cup. The Drunken Dragon, the Drunken Tiger, the Lord of Brewers, the Baron of Liquor, Drink-Like-A-Whale, Swallow-The-Ocean, Lunatic Flower, Suffering Leaf, Pleasure Grounds, Evil Horse, Drunken Laugh, Alcoholic Grief, humans and non-humans alike came from all directions. At that time the Buddha gave a complete explanation of the sermon on Saving the World through Drunken Rapture. The Great Vision Wine Buddha repeatedly gave his blessings, providing for all mankind without divisions and praising all the sages, so as to give pleasure and abolish suffering. Bleary eyes and raucous singing can purify the heart and bring eternal separation from earthly ties, so that everyone can attain perfect wisdom and enlightenment. This virtue is called *bōyūmono* ('forget grief')[16] and *sōshūshū* ('sweep away grief').[17] The flavor is named Evening Dew, and also Nectar of the Buddha's Teaching. Borrowing this wisdom from a Bodhisattva, I extinguish 'trying' and 'doing'. Especially named by the Buddha, this wine is called *hannyatō* ('liquid of wisdom')."

Mankind received this sutra in olden times; when the Wine Buddha is honored, there can be no calamity within three thousand miles, no sufferings, bad dreams, evil countenances or bad luck. Swords and staffs will not be able to cut or bruise, poisons will not cause harm, spectres will have no effect, fierce gods will not need to be worshipped, evil and malice will not be able to attack. There will be no sickness, and all can live peacefully in the countryside, witnessing the Buddha.

At the time of the earth's six great shakings,[18] the Wine Buddha appeared on earth. Holding crab's claws[19] in his left hand, he lifted a giant cup with his right hand while uttering a single roar like that of a lion. He told the Buddha, "World-honored One, I have a form of rice juice that truly makes a hundred medicines able to comfort every anguished Bodhisattva. This fragrance is the greatest in the world of men and gods: hold a great cup, fill it to the brim with rice juice and offer it to the Buddha. The fragrance extends from No-Regrets Mountain to the Three Thousand Worlds,[20] where three thousand cups have the flavor of ambrosia and the mood of self-enjoyment. The wine sings in the throat, strikes the tongue, stirs the nose, soothes the forehead and prevents grief. The Drunken Dragon, Drunken Tiger and High Sun drink together with Liu Ling and Li Po, drooling at the mouth, chasing the aromas, never losing the yearning and the warmth of this great wine. Not being able to endure the thirst for it, ultimately everyone lifts giant cups, empties them and becomes falling-down drunk. After a while, the strength of the wine bubbles up in men sleepily soaring without speaking in all directions with heaven and earth for a cushion, forgetting all things, forgetting the self, ears not hearing the clap of thunder, eyes not seeing sacred Mount T'ai. Directly entering the scenery of drunkenness, everyone can attain great joy."

The Wine Buddha also said to the Buddha, "This rice juice of mine completely abolishes thoughts of self and foolish ideas, pours over worries, fosters the inborn nature, regards equally high and low, rich and poor, joining them all together in law and truth. Opinions are lost, therefore the heart is not hindered; there is no fear, love, hate, joy or anger. Suddenly everyone is free from the fetters of earthly cares, and enters the wondrous pleasures of the drunken paradise. Thus the 365 days, four elements, 36,000 places and five senses become one. The sages of ancient dynasties depended upon this rice juice for wisdom, followed the Great Way and unified their selves. This is the way to complete enlightenment, to know the dreams of the drunken spirit. This charm for immortality, this charm for the incomparably true word can eliminate all suffering from mankind. This truth is not empty, and the magic of drunken dreams can be explained, namely:

Ryū Hakurin ya Ri Taihaku	*Liu Ling and Li Po*
sake o nomaneba	*without drinking wine*
tada no hito	*would be ordinary people—*
Yoshino akashi no	*Yoshino and Akashi's*
tsuki hana mo	*moon and flowers*
sake wa nakereba	*without sake*
tada no toko	*would be ordinary places—*
yoi yoi yoi	*drunk drunk drunk*
yoi yoi ya na	*drunk drunk, mm?*[21]

The Wine Buddha also said to the Buddha, "The meritorious virtue of the Drinker's Paradise is already well known. Long after the Buddha's death, at times of entering the world without a Buddha, when I wish all men and women to experience the peaceful joy of the Drinker's Paradise, without asking Evil Guest, Alone Sober or Banana Leaf, I guide everyone to a scenic place, prompted by painful coldness, to let them know warmth. Since olden times, if I let even one person come to the point of death without doing this for him, I cannot achieve enlightenment."

At that time the Buddha praised the Wine Buddha, saying, "Well done! Well done! Truly this is heavenly beauty, goodness and happiness!" The World-Honored One chanted in praise:

> *Worldly men are always anxious over worldly oppositions,*
> *This old man always rejoices in the companionship of sake.*
> *Wealth, success and great achievement are merely hidden in wine,*
> *Being of service or being rejected, I forget all such cares.*
> *Within complete drunkenness, months and years pass unnoticed,*
> *I stagger around not seeing even my own body.*
> *Originally the guest of green mountains and white clouds,*
> *If I die of drink, why should I care if I'm buried or not?*[22]

8. Text for Catalog No. 63.

THANKING IMPERIAL ADVISOR MENG FOR THE FRESH TEA HE HAS SENT ME
(Lu T'ung; this poem is also known as *Tea Song*)

The sun seemed fifteen feet above me, and I had fallen asleep
When an army officer knocked at the door, waking this Duke of Chou.
He tells me the Advisor has sent me a letter
On white silk with slanting folds and three official seals.
I open the missive—it is as if the Advisor and I are face to face—
And inspect by hand the Moon Brick tea, three hundred pieces of it.
I have heard that early in the year, if one goes up in the mountains,
Hibernating creatures are beginning to move and spring winds are
          starting to blow.

The Son of heaven desiring then to taste fine Yang-hsien tea,
All other plants would never dare to come to blossom first.
A gentle breeze secretly forms buds like pearls;
Before spring actually arrives, they put forth sprouts of yellow gold.
The fresh plants are gathered, the fragrant tea is fire-dried
          and pressed into bricks;

The very best, the most exquisite—no empty luxury.
Aside from the Most Honored, it is suitable for princes and dukes;
So how is it that now it has arrived at the home of a mountain man?
My bramble gate closed tight against vulgar visitors,
Wearing a cap of gauze, by myself I boil and taste the tea.
The blue smoke cloud, drawn by the wind, remains unbroken;
A white froth—floating luster—congeals in the bowl.
With bowl number one, my throat and lips are moistened;
With bowl number two, my lonely sadness is dispelled.
Bowl number three cleans out my withered bowels,
Leaving only five thousand volumes inside![23]
With bowl number four, I raise a light sweat
And all the worrisome affairs of my entire life
          evaporate through my pores.

With bowl number five, my skin and bones are purified;
With bowl number six, I commune with immortal spirits.
Bowl number seven I can barely get down:
I only feel pure wind blowing, swishing beneath my arms!
The mountains of the P'eng-lai paradise,
          where can they be found?

The Master of Jade Stream[24] wants to mount this pure wind
and go there now.
The myriad immortals on these mountains officiate
over this lowly realm;
Their position is noble and pure, beyond the stormy rains.
What do they know of the millions of beings
Tumbling from precipitous cliffs, suffering so much!
Let me question the Advisor about these sentient beings:
Ultimately, should they obtain respite, or not?[25]

---

1 Also known as Yoshida Tokushun, he lived from 1384 to 1468, and was recognized by the Shogunate with the rank of "Hō-in." See Takeoka Tomozō, ed., *Ika jinmei jiten* (Dictionary of Doctors, Tokyo, 1930).

2 Fang Shih, author of an important collection of biographies of artists and himself a fine painter and calligrapher.

3 A rare Sung dynasty compilation which survives only in fragments.

4 Also known as Yoshida Sōjun (1568-1620), he served Tokugawa Ieyasu.

5 Yoshida Munenaka (1762-1800).

6 Referring to many blessings, many years and many sons.

7 Alluding to a poem from the *Shih ching* in which the wish is expressed that a lord be "like" mountains, streams etc., in longevity, a total of nine similes.

8 Translated by Jonathan Chaves.

9 Translated by Jonathan Chaves.

10 Where the famous Buddhist layman Vimalakirti lived.

11 Lu Yu (1125-1209).

12 Translated by Jonathan Chaves.

13 A Confucian classic in which moral judgements were said to have been rendered by using certain key terms.

14 Translated by Jonathan Chaves.

15 Translated by Jonathan Chaves.

16 The name of a wine.

17 The name of another wine.

18 The Buddha's conception, birth, temptation, enlightenment, first preaching and nirvana.

19 Popular food to eat while drinking *sake*.

20 The Buddhist universe.

21 This is an extended version of the poem on Bōsai's painting of the gourd (No. 39). For still another version, see Nishikawa Gyokko, "Bōsai Sensei itsuji" (Anecdotes about Bōsai), Part 2, *Kōzuke oyobi Kōzukejin*, No. 83 (March, 1924) pp. 41-42.

22 Another version of this poem was quoted earlier.

23 A scholar was said to have thousands of books in his stomach.

24 Lu T'ung himself.

25 Translated by Jonathan Chaves.

Appendix B: SEALS OF BŌSAI

Notes:

1 When seals appear on reliable dated works, the range of dates is given after the reading of the seal. Please note that the seals may have been used in other years as well.

2 A number of doubtful works bear seal impressions not given here. At times they are entirely different seal designs, but more often they are variant versions of known seals, including numbers 1, 2, 3, 10, 11, 13, 16, 21, 25, 27, 28, 29, 31, 35, 37, 38, 39, and 42. Seal number 31 has the greatest number of variants.

3 Bosai's seals seem to have been defaced or destroyed at his death except for numbers 1 and 19, which were given to Nishina Hakkoku.

4 *Calligraphy by Joseph Tsenti Chang.*

1 Chōkō no in, 1820; later given to Hakkoku.

2 Zenshin, 1819-1824.

3 Chōkō Shi-in, 1794-1820.

4 Kameda Chōkō, 1824.

5 Shōbidō (Rose Grotto), 1807-1815.

6 Bōsai, 1808-1810.

7 Eihoku Chitsufu.

8 Kameda Kō in, 1802.

弟孔
子門

9 Kōmon deshi
(Confucian
student), 1794.

狂鵬
叟齋

10 Bōsai kyōsō (Bōsai
the crazy old man).

之長
記興

11 Chōkō no ki,
1817-1824.

之長
印興

12 Chōkō no in,
1802-1805.

間鵬
人齋

13 Bōsai kanjin
(Bōsai at leisure),
1802-1809.

散非
人寶

14 Hihō sanjin, 1821.

縣糟
子丘

15 Sōkyū kenshi
(Courtier of Wine-
dregs Hill).

尚麴
書部

16 Kikubu Shōsho,
1808-1823.

華鋪優
菴羅曇

17 Yūdon Hachira
Ka-an (Fig Flower
Studio),
1818-1823.

堂善
印身

18 Zenshindō in.

閒天
人許

19 Tenkyo kanjin (The
man allowed
leisure by heaven),
1808; given to
Hakkoku.

清兩
風袖

20 Ryōsode seifū
(Both sleeves in
the pure wind).

酒爰

21 Shu-in (Retired to
wine), 1802-1810.

鵬
齋

22 Bōsai.

墨農

23 Bokunō (Ink
farmer),
1814-1824.

風關
顛東
生第
　一

24 Kantō dai-ichi
fūtensei (The
greatest fool in the
Kantō area), 1818-
1823.

閒鵬
人齋

25 Bōsai kanjin,
1794-1820.

龍

26 (?) ryū (?), 1802.

浪海
人東

27 Kaitō rōjin (The
man floating in the
Eastern Ocean),
1807-1817.

醉太
民平

28 Taihei suishi (The
great peace
drunkard),
1807-1810.

醉太
民平

29 Taihei suishi,
1821-1824.

藝公

30 Kōgei,
1802-1805.

齋鵬

31 Bōsai,
1820-1824.

人庠下
仙界

32 Gekaitaku sennin
(Hermit criticized
by the world),
1818-1824.

老金
鈍杉

33 Kanasugi rōdon
(The old dullard of
Kanasugi),
1808-1815.

墨
農

34 Bokunō,
1809-1820.

鵬
齋

35 Bōsai.

壇
穉
史

36 Shōheki shi
(History written on
a wall).

醒
狂

37 Seikyō (Sober but
crazy),
1803-1811.

善
身

38 Zenshin,
1815-1823.

鵬
齋

39 Bōsai.

鵬

40 Bōsai.

鵬齋

善身堂

齋鵬

41 Bōsai,
1807-1824.

42 Zenshindō,
1820-1824.

43 Bōsai.

齋鵬

44 Bōsai.

長興

45 Chōkō,
1810-1820.

鵬齋

46 Bōsai, 1817-1823.

長興

47 Chōkō.

2 - 1 = 1

The m&m's® Subtraction Book

Barbara Barbieri McGrath

Charlesbridge

M&M'S® candies are tasty—that's a fact.

You'll see for yourself once you learn to subtract!

To see how it's done, simply read on.

Just learn to subtract until they are gone!

Are M&M'S® candies in here? There's no doubt.

But it's zero you see, until they're poured out.

Zero is an important number, even though it has no value.

Zero means there is nothing of something.

It's a full bag! Let's take some away.
For learning subtraction, this is the day!

Open the bag and spread out the candies. Sort them so that you have six groups of different colors. Each group is called a set.

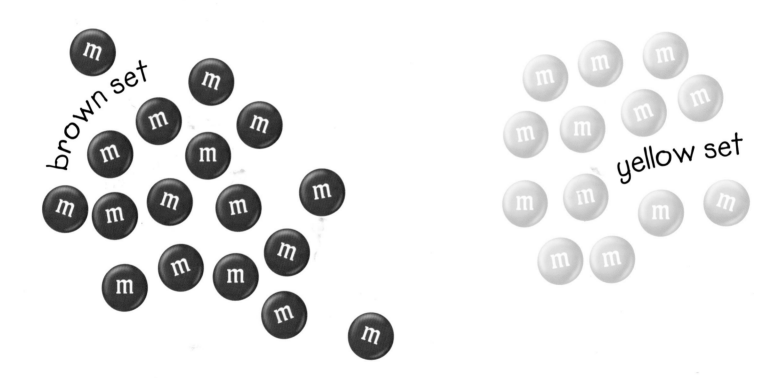

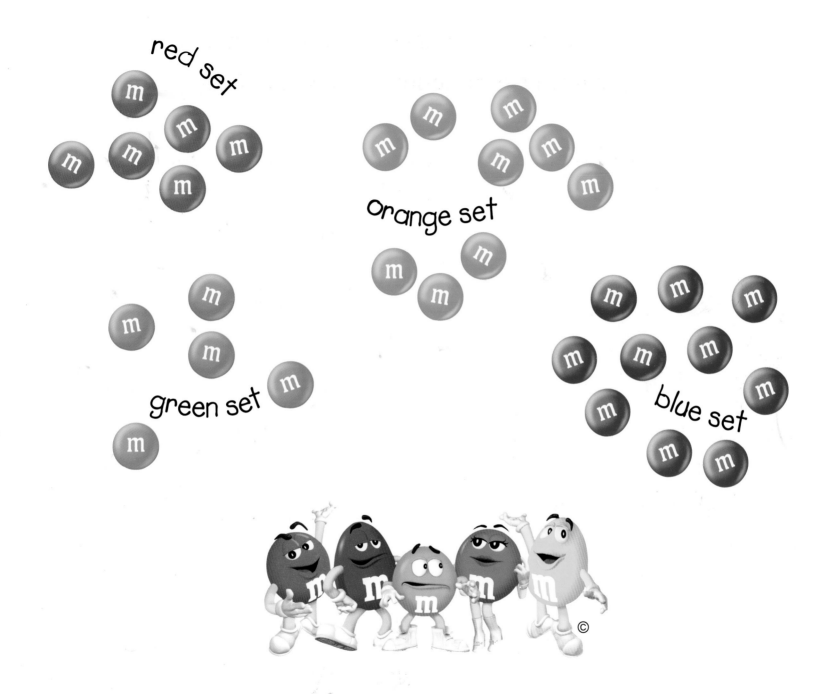

red set

orange set

green set

blue set

7

When doing subtraction, it's fun to compare.
Which set has less than another set there?

You can think of subtracting as comparing different sets of objects. Find out which color set has more than another. Which has fewer?

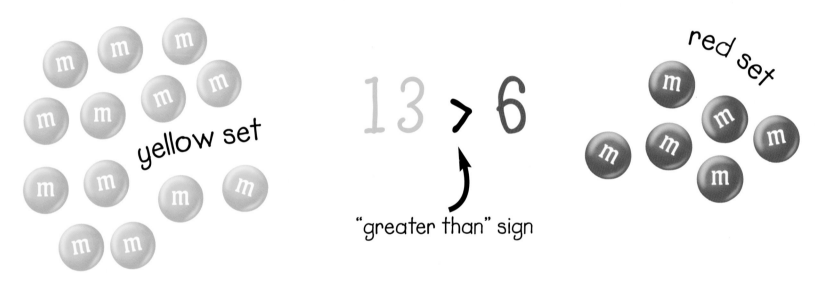

yellow set

13 > 6

"greater than" sign

red set

There are more yellow than red ones.
We can write it this way:

Yellow > Red

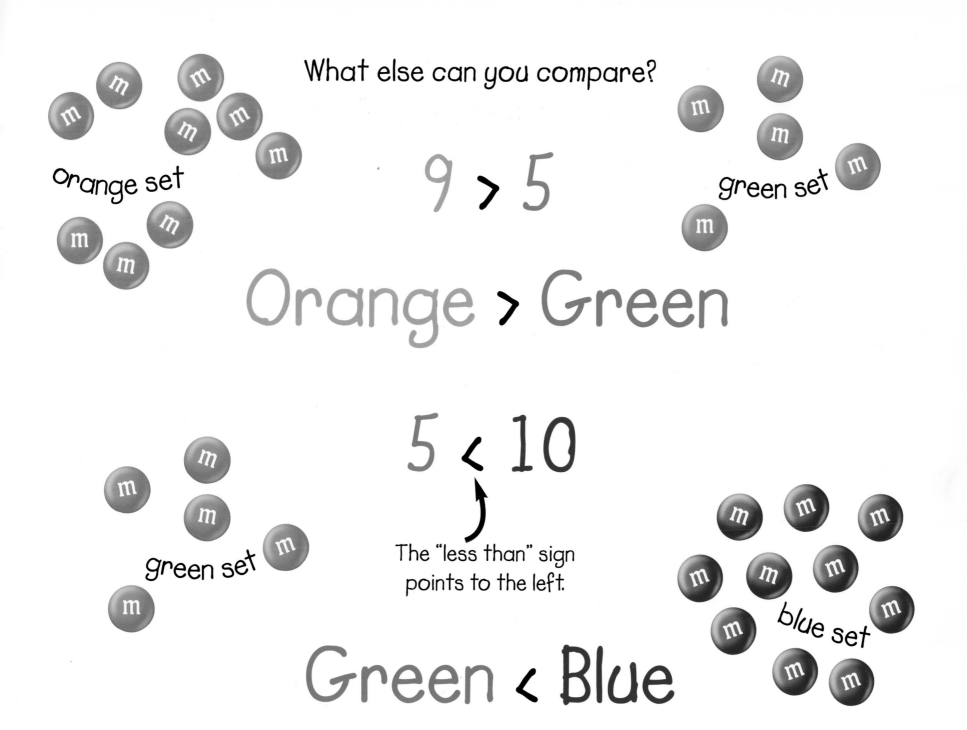

What else can you compare?

orange set

9 > 5

green set

Orange > Green

5 < 10

green set

The "less than" sign points to the left.

Green < Blue

blue set

Let's try our first problem. It's easy—you'll see!
We'll look for the difference—what the answer will be.

An equation is a number sentence. Let's try writing one.

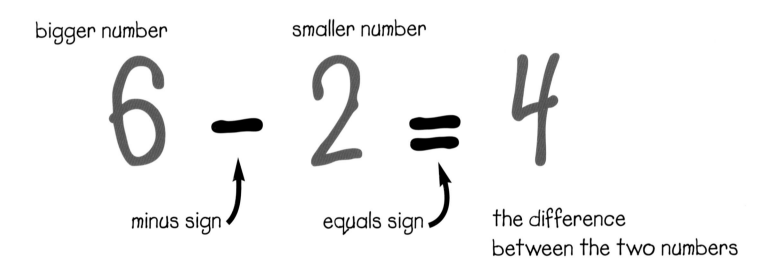

bigger number   smaller number

$$6 - 2 = 4$$

minus sign   equals sign   the difference
between the two numbers

In subtraction, the smaller number is taken away from the larger number to get
the answer. The bigger number goes on the left. The smaller number goes on
the right, after the minus sign. The answer in a subtraction problem is called
the difference. The difference comes after the equals sign.

Start with the six red candies. Take two candies away.

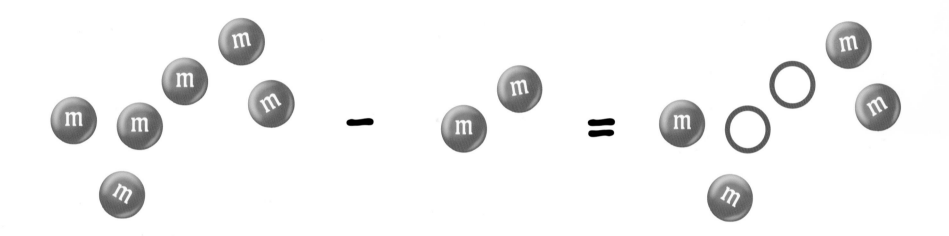

You say the sentence this way:

Six minus two equals four.

Write some equations. They'll help to explain:
What's missing? What's left? How many remain?

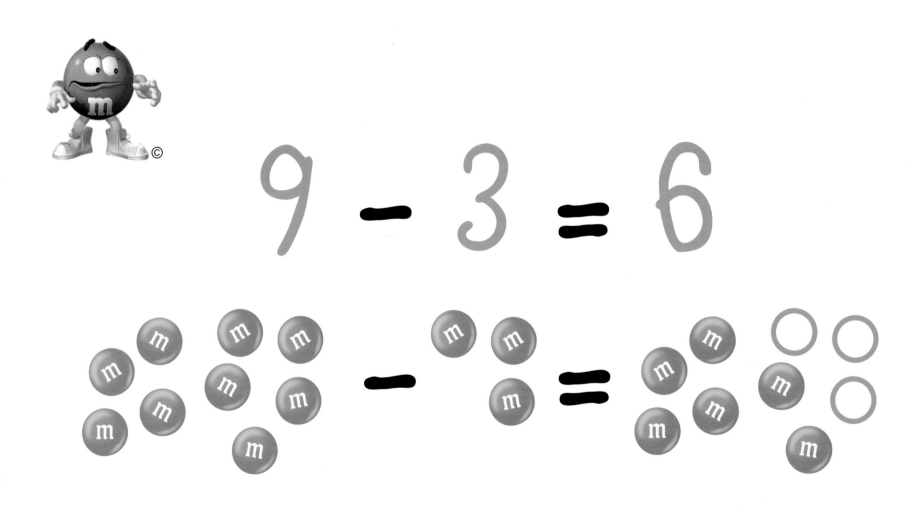

$$9 - 3 = 6$$

5 − 4 = 1

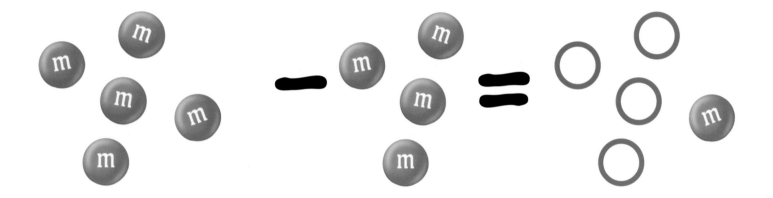

13

Now write the equation with the big number on top. Take some away. It's so hard to stop!

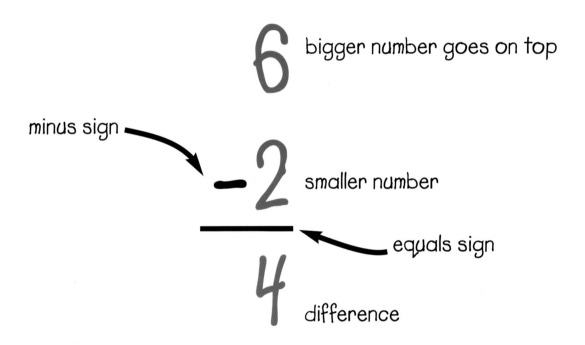

6 bigger number goes on top

minus sign

-2 smaller number

equals sign

4 difference

Here the subtraction problem is set up a different way. When subtracting a number greater than zero, the answer is always less than the number you subtracted from.

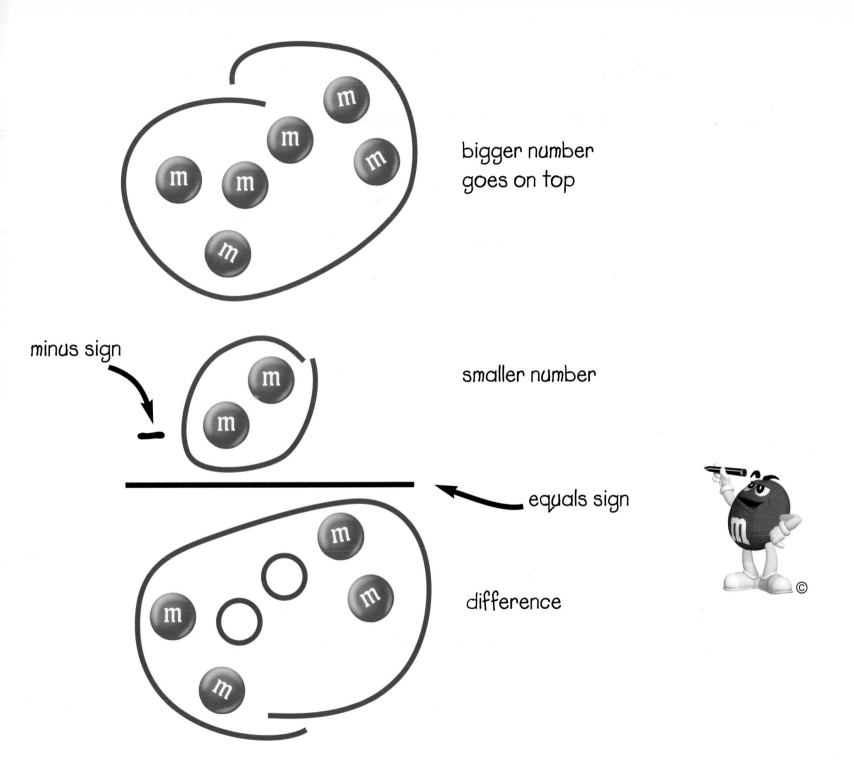

bigger number
goes on top

minus sign

smaller number

equals sign

difference

15

Up and down gives subtraction a whole different look.
The bottom from the top—that's what you took.

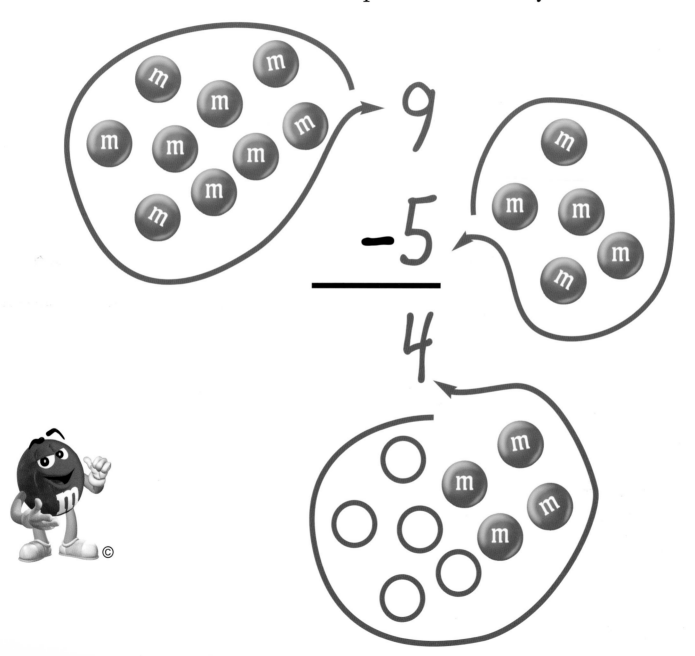

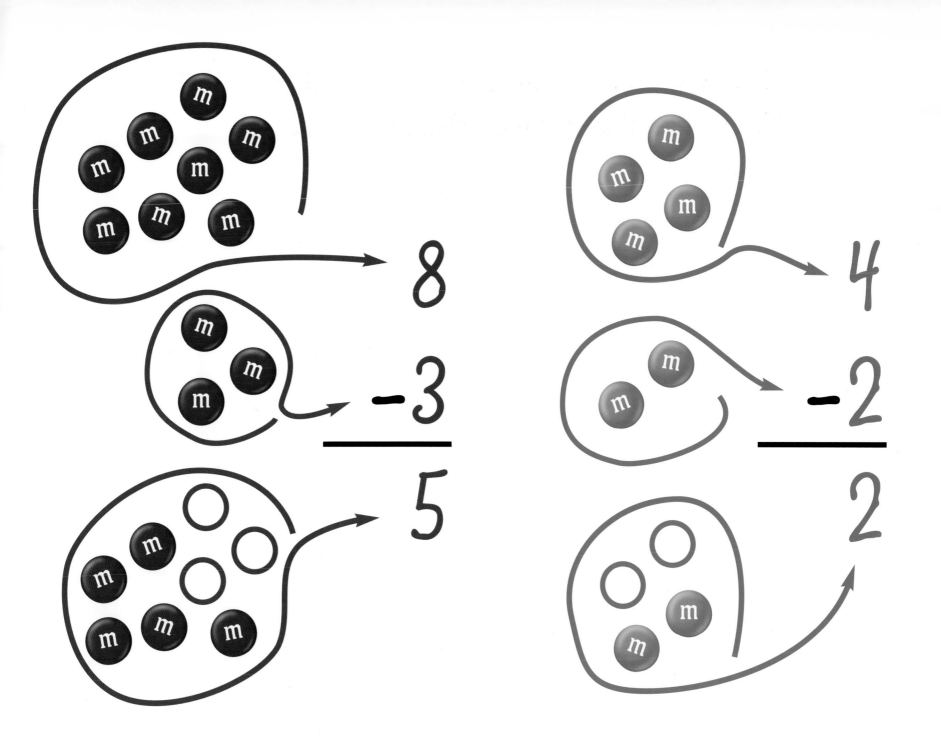

8

−3
_____
5

4

−2
_____
2

Subtracting starts with how many you had.
To see if you're right, you just have to add.

The opposite of subtraction is addition. It's always a good
idea to check your answers in math. In subtraction, it's easy—
just add your answer to the number you took away.
Does that add up to the number you started with?
Then you did it right!

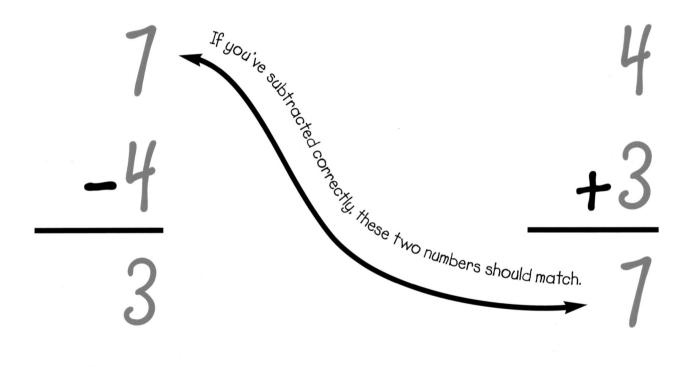

7
−4
―――
3

If you've subtracted correctly, these two numbers should match.

4
+3
―――
7

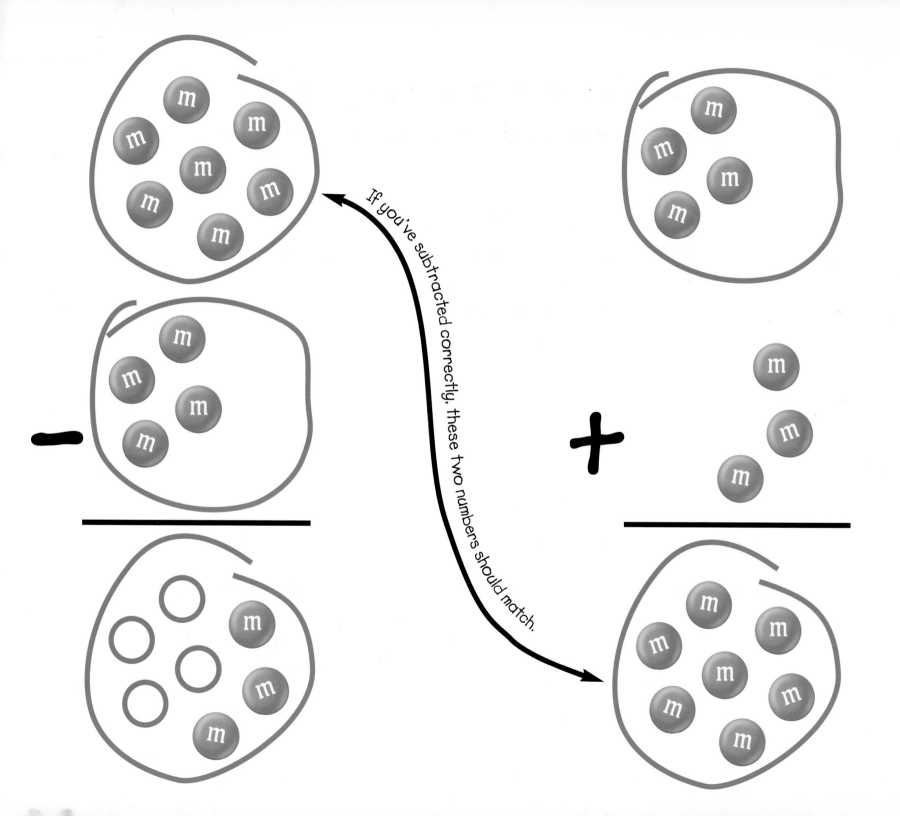

If you've subtracted correctly, these two numbers should match.

19

When subtracting large numbers, you will see:
Ones, tens, hundreds—place value is key.

The numbers 0 through 9 are called digits.

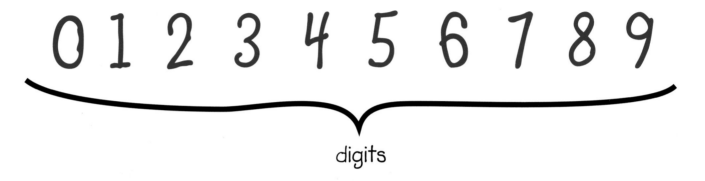

0 1 2 3 4 5 6 7 8 9

digits

Bigger numbers from 10 to 99 use two of those digits:
one digit in the ones column and one digit in the tens column.

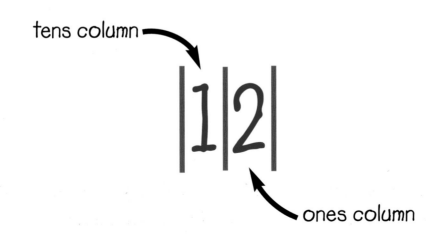

tens column

|1|2|

ones column

To subtract double-digit numbers, you simply subtract the numbers in the ones column and the numbers in the tens column.

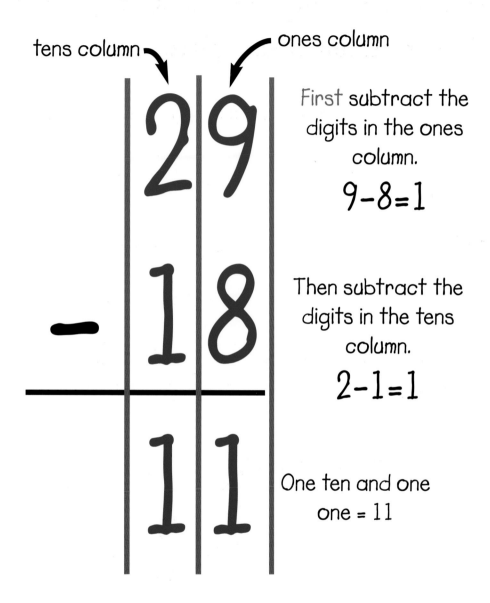

tens column

ones column

First subtract the digits in the ones column.

$9-8=1$

Then subtract the digits in the tens column.

$2-1=1$

One ten and one one = 11

Since the larger number is on top, it's easy. Nine minus eight is one. Two minus one is one. The answer is eleven.

21

It's fun to practice when you learn something new.

Let's try some more problems—you know what to do!

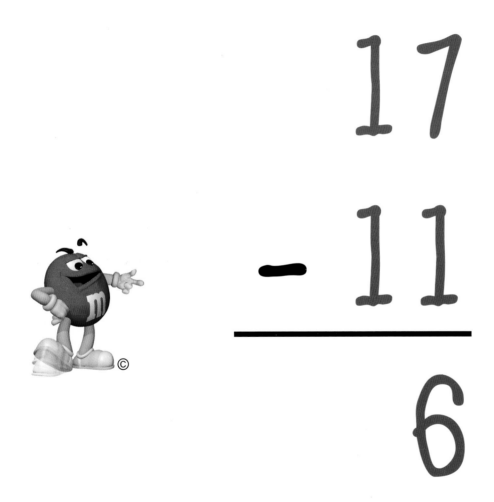

$$\begin{array}{r} 17 \\ -\ 11 \\ \hline 6 \end{array}$$

$$\begin{array}{r} 24 \\ -\ 13 \\ \hline 11 \end{array} \qquad \begin{array}{r} 32 \\ -\ 20 \\ \hline 12 \end{array}$$

For two-digit numbers, don't worry! Don't fret!
You'll just have to borrow—let's see what you get.

m Thirty-seven is larger than nineteen. But in the ones column, the larger number is on the bottom.

m To subtract, you must borrow a ten from the tens column. Now there are only two tens left in the tens column.

m The seven becomes seventeen.

m Seventeen ones minus nine ones equals eight ones.

m Two tens minus one ten is one ten, so the difference is eighteen.

How many more can you do?

24

First, borrow a ten from the tens column.

Second, add the ten to the ones column.

$$
\begin{array}{r}
{}^{2}\cancel{3}\,{}^{17}\cancel{7} \\
-\ 19 \\
\hline
18
\end{array}
$$

Third, subtract the numbers in the ones column.

17-9=8

Fourth, subtract the numbers in the tens column.

2-1=1

candies are left!

You've mastered subtraction, so give a big cheer!
These M&M'S® candies will soon disappear!

Sets

brown set  13

red set 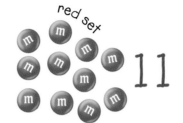 11

 5
green set

 4
blue set

orange set

Greater than

9 > 5

Orange > Green

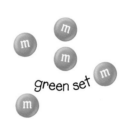
green set

Less than

5 < 10

Green < Blue

blue set

Single digit

9 - 3 = 6

$$\begin{array}{r} 9 \\ - 5 \\ \hline 4 \end{array}$$

Double digit

$$\begin{array}{r} 17 \\ - 11 \\ \hline 6 \end{array}$$

Double digit / borrowing

$$\begin{array}{r} {}^{2}\cancel{3}{}^{17} \\ - 19 \\ \hline 18 \end{array}$$

26

Love to my brother John, who is never minus an encouraging word!

—B. B. M.

Text copyright © 2005 by Barbara Barbieri McGrath
Illustrations copyright © 2005 by Charlesbridge Publishing
All rights reserved, including the right of reproduction in whole or in part in any form.
Charlesbridge and colophon are registered trademarks of Charlesbridge Publishing, Inc.

Published by Charlesbridge
85 Main Street
Watertown, MA 02472
(617) 926-0329
www.charlesbridge.com

Library of Congress Cataloging-in-Publication Data
McGrath, Barbara Barbieri, 1954-
    The M&M'S® brand subtraction book / Barbara Barbieri McGrath.
        p. cm.
    ISBN 1-57091-358-7 (reinforced for library use)
    ISBN 1-57091-359-5 (softcover)
1. Subtraction—Juvenile literature. I. Title.
QA115.M387 2005
513.2'12—dc22   2004003309

Printed in Korea
(hc) 10 9 8 7 6 5 4 3 2 1
(sc) 10 9 8 7 6 5 4 3 2 1

Display type set in Hip Hop and text type set in Adobe Caslon
Printed and bound by Sung In Printing, South Korea
Production supervision by Brian G. Walker
Designed by Susan Mallory Sherman

™/® & © M&M'S, M and the M&M'S Characters are trademarks of Mars, Incorporated and its affiliates.
© Mars, Inc. Manufactured and distributed under license by Charlesbridge Publishing.

27